55,

Underemployed,

and

Faking Normal

Your Guide to a Better Life

Elizabeth White

Simon & Schuster

NEW YORK LONDON TORONTO SYDNEY NEW DELHI

Simon & Schuster
1230 Avenue of the Americas
New York, NY 10020

First Simon & Schuster hardcover edition January 2019

SIMON & SCHUSTER and colophon are registered trademarks
of Simon & Schuster, Inc.

For information about special discounts for bulk purchases,
please contact Simon & Schuster Special Sales at 1-866-506-1949
or business@simonandschuster.com.

The Simon & Schuster Speakers Bureau can bring authors to your
live event. For more information or to book an event, contact the
Simon & Schuster Speakers Bureau at 1-866-248-3049
or visit our website at www.simonspeakers.com.

Interior design by Paul Dippolito

All websites noted in this book were accurate when the book went to press.

Manufactured in the United States of America

1 3 5 7 9 10 8 6 4 2

Library of Congress Cataloging-in-Publication Data is available.

ISBN 978-1-5011-9680-5
ISBN 978-1-5011-9684-3 (ebook)

In loving memory of my dad, George B. White, Jr.
and
My mom, Dorothy K. White

Contents

Author's Note: About Me

I am standing in the line to buy groceries. A stranger approaches. "I know you. I know you," he says, this man I've never seen before. "Aren't you that woman who's . . ." and his voice trails off. I can see he's searching for just the right word. "Who's broke," I say, holding his gaze. His face lights up. "That's it, that's right," he says, heartily shaking my hand. "I saw you on TV."

Being the poster child for broke baby boomers was not on my bucket list. Even now I still cringe when I listen to some of the interviews I've done or think about what I've revealed about myself. By nature I am a private person, reserved, not someone who would put all their business in the street.

I grew up in a two-parent household, one of three adored children. My father was a career officer in the army. We moved around a lot. I counted fourteen moves in twelve years, including to places like Libya, Italy, and Germany. I remember being in seventh grade on three continents. I got used to being the new kid in class.

Even as a little girl I knew there was a big difference between what I experienced at home and what I experienced in the world outside. In the early 1960s I was often the only little black girl in my elementary school class. I remember not understanding why no one ever picked me for the soccer or volleyball team even though I was a decent athlete. I was the default choice, picked last after the boy with the bulletproof glasses and the girl who smelled like she peed in the bed.

I remember at thirteen going to my first dance at the local teen club and neither the white boys nor the black boys asked me to dance. Back in those days beauty standards were strict. There were no Lupita Nyong'os gracing the cover of fashion magazines. You were either paint-by-numbers pretty or you weren't. You either fit or you didn't. And with my dark skin and rounded African features, I never did.

Eventually, I stopped trying and focused on achievement instead, receiving a BA from Oberlin College and an MA from the Johns Hopkins School of Advanced International Studies. I worked summers in Paris and the Gambia in West Africa. I was in my early to mid-twenties and life was full of promise and good things to come. Back then we boomers were still the youngest people in the room.

After spending so much time overseas, it's no surprise that I ended up at the World Bank. I did not have to hide my ethnicity there. My natural hair and diamond nose post fit in easily among all the turbans, saris, and caftans. I was thirty at the time and earned enough money to buy the town house I still live in today some thirty-four years later.

After about five years at the World Bank, I jumped at the chance to take a sabbatical and go back to school. Many of my World Bank colleagues had PhDs. I didn't. I remember thinking an MBA was the next-best thing. I was thrilled when Harvard accepted me.

I caught the entrepreneurial bug at Harvard. I had never considered becoming one before then. Some entrepreneurs are born, but not me. Truth be told, my mom bought all my Girl Scout cookies! But at Harvard I listened to classmates, mostly men, talk about becoming captains of industry. I remember thinking, *I am as smart as that guy over there. Why can't I create something?*

And my retail business was born. Well, not right away. I stayed at the World Bank another few years, getting my ducks in a row. I then joined my mother, who was co-owner in the business.

Being a business owner and entrepreneur was a wild ride and humbling too. It was my first time selling widgets instead of services. I was used to working in environments where a great report could buy you months of goodwill. In retail, it's what have you done for me lately. Big sales days didn't carry over. Each day was a new grind. Each day started at zero.

There was also a certain status to working for the World Bank. Suddenly, out on my own, I was chief cook and bottle washer, running some start-up no one had ever heard of. At the World Bank I just showed up and did the work. I didn't worry about payroll or keeping the lights on. But now my mother and I were creating a business from the ground up: the infrastructure and systems, vetting the suppliers (many from Africa), negotiating store leases, and hiring and training staff. It was a ton of work—I mean a straight vertical lift—but also possibly the most fun I've ever had "on a job."

Besides, I wasn't alone. It would have been insane to launch a retail business with no experience. My mother and I had a great team of retail professionals helping us, some giants in their field, with twenty or more years of retail experience.

So it was devastating, eight years later, when the business failed. We had cash flow problems and struggled to keep some stores stocked. We were sourcing from dozens of small artisan suppliers and couldn't get the quantity of products we needed at the right price and quality. We raised money, but not enough. It's called "skin in the game" when you add your money to what your investors have put in. After eight years in I had emptied out my savings.

I was forty-seven and back out in the job market. I wasn't overly worried. I had my background, work history at some prestigious organizations, and degrees from Hopkins and Harvard. You'd think all that would count for something.

I never did land a real nine-to-five job but did eventually get a "short-term" consultancy. It was supposed to be for about seven months but ended up lasting for seven years. Three years into that first consultancy, I got a second one from another institution, also "short-term." But, like the first one, it was renewed several times. The combined income from those two assignments put me solidly in the six figures.

We didn't call it "gig work" back then, but that's what it was. I didn't have to go into the office every day, and I paid for my own benefits. I remember liking the work and flexibility. I was also able to start building back my savings.

Then the Great Recession of 2008–2009 hit. Both institutions I worked for were in retrenchment mode. I lost both consulting jobs within six months. My income dropped to zero. I was fifty-five and unemployed.

I still had my great background, but something had changed. My phone wasn't ringing. Recruiters weren't calling me back for interviews. I was filling out dozens of online applications and not hearing back at all.

Months turned into two years. Here and there I'd get a little assignment. I edited documents, did some training, worked as an adjunct professor at a local university—small jobs that didn't pay anything close to what I was used to making.

With nothing to speak of coming in, I was running through what was left of my savings. Thank God, I managed to hang on to my house. I was within walking distance of everything and had lived there so long that my mortgage was low and very affordable.

Finally, I was hired. It was a great job but in a toxic environment. I was back out in the street in two years and pushing sixty.

At sixty it was crickets. I remember going an eight-month stretch without a single callback from a recruiter—not even an inquiry.

And my once robust network had been decimated. People had moved on, retired, died even. When I was younger, I used to hear about assignments before they were posted publicly. Now I was totally out of the loop.

It had never been this bad before. I was stressed-out and scared, but trying to hold it together. I was still having coffee with people, attending professional networking events, going to hear speakers in my field to stay current. I was doing all the stuff that used to work for me in the past.

But nothing was happening. I started to notice friends in the same boat, also trying to keep up appearances. By now I had learned to read the "faking normal" signs: that panicked look when the check arrives and you're terrified you're going to be asked to split a bill you can't afford; looking a tad rough around the edges because you're going long between appointments to conserve the little cash you have; that vacant, faraway look of the "formerly" and "used to be."

A small group of us began to talk, to tell the truth about what was happening to us. Men and women friends shared their stories. They were surprising similar. All of us were fifty-five or older, well educated, with a history of career choice and good incomes. And then the bottom fell out with no ladder to climb back up.

At a particularly low point I wrote an essay called "You Know Her." It described what it *feels* like to land here after a lifetime of work. I have included it right after this personal note.

I sent it around and eventually it made its way onto the PBS Facebook page. "Likes" started pouring in, some 11,000 in three days and over 1,000 comments. I was stunned. I had written a composite essay just about me and my friends, or so I thought. And yet, here were all these other people responding with "Me too."

I read every comment. And the stories had common themes. I was struck by how remarkably similar they were. It didn't matter whether you were white-collar or blue-collar. The common thread was being in your forties, fifties, or sixties, underemployed or unemployed, facing a "Don't want you" job market and downward mobility often for the first time. Many wrote about feeling shell-shocked, ashamed, alone, and scared about the future.

People found my email address online and started to write me directly—hundreds of people. Most were short notes thanking me for raising this issue, but dozens were long letters describing what had happened to them personally.

I wrote back, and friendships have grown out of the correspondence. You will meet some of these friends in this book. I've also met many others for coffee who live in the Washington metro area or were visiting from out of town. I share insights from those conversations too.

All these stories led me to ask bigger questions. I have the background to look at the data and was astonished by what I learned. As a country we are facing a retirement income crisis of mega-proportions. It is America's big denial issue, what a friend of mine calls the "loud silence."

But there are signs that this is changing. A small but growing chorus is sounding the alarm and making recommendations about a way forward. Often these recommendations take the long view, with detailed proposals for averting a retirement savings crisis for people today in their twenties and thirties.

This is a necessary step, for sure.

But what about the millions of Americans in their fifties and sixties living this retirement income crisis today? What happens to us in the meantime?

I wrote 55, Underemployed, and Faking Normal to bring urgent attention and national focus to the millions of older adults living in that "meantime." I wrote it because policy prescriptions and other measures that address this retirement income crisis should not and must not skip over people living it now.

This is also the book I wish I had had when I was circling the drain and going through the worst of my own personal financial crisis. My family and friends, old and new, have been the scaffolding that held me up. I've learned a lot from people who've been navigating these choppy retirement income waters much longer than I have. From them I got context, perspective, and some good life hacks that helped me get my mojo back. I may be broke but I am not broken. And I want that for you, too . . . in the meantime.

Preface: You Know Her

You know her.

She is in your friendship circle, hidden in plain sight. Her clothes are still impeccable, bought in the good years when she was still making money.

To look at her, you would not know that her electricity was cut off last week for nonpayment or that she meets the eligibility requirements for food stamps.

But if you paid attention, you would see the sadness in her eyes, hear that hint of fear in her otherwise self-assured voice.

These days she buys the $1.99 trial-size jug of Tide to make ends meet. You didn't know laundry detergent came in that size.

You invite her to the same expensive restaurants that the two of you have always enjoyed, but she orders mineral water now with a twist of lemon instead of the $12 glass of Chardonnay.

She is frugal in her menu choices, meticulous, counting every penny in her head. She demurs dividing the table bill evenly to cover desserts, designer coffees, and second and third glasses of wine she did not consume.

She is tired of trying to keep up appearances. Faking normal is wearing her out.

There are no media stories about her. Her slide out of the middle class is not sensational enough.

A friend says that she's broke, not poor, and that there's a difference. She lives without cable, her gym membership, or nail appointments. She's discovered that she can do her own hair.

She has no retirement savings, no nest egg. She exhausted that long ago. There is no expensive condo from which to draw equity and no husband to back her up.

Months of slow pay and no pay have decimated her credit. Bill collectors call her constantly, reading verbatim from a script, expressing polite sympathy for her plight before demanding payment arrangements that she can't possibly meet.

Friends wonder privately how someone so well educated could be in economic free fall. She is still as talented as ever and as smart as a whip, but her work is sketchy now, mostly on-and-off consulting gigs.

Friends hear about this and that assignment but can't remember when she had a real job. At fifty-five, she has learned how to fake cheeriness and to appear to be engaged, but her phone doesn't ring with opportunities anymore.

She doesn't remember exactly when it stopped. But she cannot deny now having entered the uncertain world of "formerly" and "used to be." In the face of mega-generational shifts, she's not sure anymore where she belongs.

What she does know is that dozens of online job applications seem to disappear into a black hole. She's convinced that employers have set their online job recruitment algorithms to reject anyone who graduated before 1995.

She wonders what is to become of her. She is facing a work-for-life proposition. So far her health has held up, but her body aches—or is it her spirit?

Homeless women used to be invisible to her, but she appraises them now with curious eyes, wondering if their stories started like hers.

Chapter 1

Lost, Ashamed, and Shell-shocked

And when you're totally honest about your health and finan-cial situation to family and friends, the pack seems to thin out rather quickly.

—Robert

"You Know Her" first appeared on PBS's website *Next Avenue* in the winter of 2015 and again in May 2016. It is a composite of my own experiences and those of many of my baby boomer–age friends. I wrote it because I didn't see myself in the articles on retirement that I was reading in the popular press.

No one I knew was traveling the world or buying condos in Costa Rica. As cool as the idea sounded, we could not afford to redefine retirement on "our own terms." Our dreams of launching fulfilling second- and third-act careers were put on hold so that we could take part-time jobs that would pay the bills. Many of us were facing a work-for-life proposition, one major crisis away from insolvency.

My article struck a chord with people who saw the woman I described in their friends, their sisters, their daughters, and them-selves. They used words like *lost, ashamed, shell-shocked,* and *secret sisterhood* to describe how they were feeling.

They reminded me that "faking normal" happens to men too.

We endure what is happening to us in silence and often alone, too embarrassed or ashamed to talk about it. We assume we are small in number—that we are the only ones facing serious, life-altering financial challenges. We fake normal as best we can, trying to keep up appearances as the floor collapses underneath us.

Well, it turns out that we are not alone at all: there are millions of us.

Very few boomers have managed to save the fifteen to twenty times[1] their annual salaries financial experts tell us we need to maintain our current standard of living.

How bad is it? According to the SCEPA Retirement Equity Lab, the median retirement savings for near retirees in the top 10 percent of earners in the US is $200,000; for the middle 40 percent of earners, it's $60,000; and for the bottom half, it's zero.[2] The median retirement account balance for all near retirees ages fifty-five to sixty-four is only $15,000.

You do the math. If we make it to age sixty-five in good health, there's a good chance that we'll live for another twenty years.[3] I don't have to tell you that's a long runway if you're broke. We're facing a massive retirement savings shortfall with millions of us looking at downward mobility, and millions more are at risk of living in poverty or near poverty.

Doom and Gloom Disempower Us

I am writing this book for us.

But I am not writing from a place of doom and gloom. Doom and gloom disempower us. Instead, this book focuses on how we can regain control over our lives in this new environment of financial vulnerability. How do we throw open the curtains and let the light in after months or years of apprehension and worries?

First, we must arm ourselves with facts. Right now our shame, embarrassment, and fear keep us in silos, disconnected, isolated, and silent. There is power in numbers.

According to AARP, the fifty-plus segment of the population consists of some 111 million consumers spending $7.6 trillion annually on goods and services.[4] In fact, we make nearly half of all the purchases in entertainment and apparel and account for 55 percent of the sales of consumer packaged goods.

When a segment of this size starts pumping the brakes on its spending, it ain't pretty. It's what happens when tens of millions of us stop shopping beyond basic necessities, start keeping that eight-year-old Chevy and taking our coffee to work in a thermos, and stop buying clothes, eating out, and going on vacation.

Not that belt tightening is necessarily a bad thing. But in our consumer-driven economy, it can't be a good thing when boomers, one of the country's key drivers of growth and jobs, start curbing their spending across the board.

A Tribe Called Aging

It's easy to dismiss this retirement income crisis as just some pesky little boomer problem. But it's way bigger than that. Boomers are just first to confront these economic challenges in such large numbers. Millennials, facing a future of lower income, unsteady work, disappearing pensions, and a trillion-plus dollars in outstanding student loan debt, are in lockstep right behind us.[5]

> *I turned thirty in October. From what I read in the press, you'd think eating all that avocado toast is why I can't afford a house.*
>
> —Maryanne

Many of the same structural issues that have adversely impacted boomers—disappearing pensions, flat and falling wages, sharply escalating costs in health care, housing, and education—are also hurting millennials and Gen Xers. My friend Marc has it right when he says we are all members of "a tribe called aging."

We Need Our Business Leaders to Step Up

Thanks to public health and medical advances, the hundred-year life is just around the corner. That's the good news. The bad news is that millions of Americans will be financing this longevity bonus with a much smaller nest egg. And a long life—broke, with no resources to cover even basic expenses—is nothing to be thrilled about.[6]

We hear a lot about the longevity economy these days both as a huge market opportunity and for its potential to deliver all kinds of goodies for older adults. But from what I can tell, the focus is not on supplying affordable options to boomers in financial jeopardy. To the extent that marketers focus on the fifty-plus demographic at all, aside from medical devices, affluent boomers are the prize. Much of the buzz is around fulfilling their needs and wants for luxury housing, entertainment, high-end travel, and the like.

Business is not yet producing many products and services to address the needs of financially strapped older adults, the broke and near broke baby boomers, and the tens of millions of younger adults on the same path. This is why we need our business leaders, marketers, and product developers to step up. We should be asking them what is your fifty-plus strategy and how do you plan to serve a fifty-and-over demographic accustomed to living well but now on a budget.

We Need to Mobilize

We who are living this retirement- and preretirement-income crisis must know that we exist and begin to convene and connect with one another, to tell our truths, and to share information and resources. This book aims to help facilitate that conversation.

We also have to stop believing that what happened to us is our "own darn fault" when in reality it's baked into a broken retirement security system that is stacked against most Americans from the jump.

And we have to let go of the thought that help is on the way. The cavalry is not coming to rescue us—not anytime soon, anyway.

There's a big disconnect in Washington. At a time when Americans need more help, not less, a lot of policy makers are threatening to cut social security benefits and Medicare.

In the meantime, we're going to have to save ourselves. Some of us have already started down this road. This book is about how we can learn from one another and share what we know.

It's about the practical steps we can take to secure ourselves in our fourth quarter. It focuses on what we can do from where we sit—and on the resources and changes in our mind-sets needed to get us there.

It asks us to consider what matters to us now, at this age and stage. What lifestyle goals are realistic? What are we willing to give up? And what *must* we give up?

We boomers are too old for hollow reassurances. The truth is that most of us will not get through this next phase of life unscathed. There is no magic wand to make everything like it once was; there are no blanket solutions.

The Silver Lining in "Smalling Up"

In the looming retirement-income crisis, I also see a silver lining. The economics of aging is forcing millions of us to live more frugally and to redefine what is enough. We're cutting back, downsizing, and rethinking how we live, work, and play.

But the problem right now is that, to most of us, downsizing looks like deprivation and loss.

And we hate it.

Small is not beautiful. It's living in a shoe box without windows or Wi-Fi and paying $1,800 per month for the privilege.

Nobody wants that.

But what if we could flip the script? What if we could take the economic turmoil of forced downsizing and come out better—not because we accommodated the chaos but because we used the chaos to go where we needed to go in the first place?

I call this idea "smalling up," and it's where the retirement-income crisis and the sustainability movement intersect.

I believe that more of us could embrace small if it were well designed, efficient, sustainable, and affordable—if, for example, our tiny apartment was airy and bright and looked out onto a beautiful courtyard, if it were well-appointed (think grown-up version of Ikea) but with sturdier furniture and comfort-height seating (and, yes, ditch the bunk beds), and if it had the basic services and amenities that we need as we age.

You get the picture.

In other words, if we're going to have to downsize, why can't we "small up" and do more with less as a path to a more sustainable way of living? Why can't we have more beautifully designed, space-saving homes and furniture made of eco-friendly materials? And why can't they be affordable and available in the mass market?

The economics of aging may well force us in this direction. But isn't this where we should be heading anyway to secure our futures and those of our children and grandchildren?

And please—pu*leeze*—don't tell us there is no demand. We're old enough to remember when Detroit automakers thought there was no appetite for gasoline-sipping, fuel-efficient cars. And we all know how that turned out.

Making Our Paths by Walking

This book culls wisdom from boomers navigating the path ahead. It is a first step for us to look beyond our immediate surroundings and circumstances to what is possible in the new normal.

It is the book to read before you embark on one of those retirement- or preretirement-planning workshops or register online for a get-back-on-track webinar that only reminds you of how far behind you are. And consider starting with this book before you attend yet another stand-around networking event that leaves you feeling worse about where you've landed, not better.

What you've told me is that, in your present state of mind, you can't take advantage of these opportunities. Stuck in your own story, all you hear is "waa, waa, waa!"

55, Underemployed, and Faking Normal aims to unstick us and start us across the bridge to making the life changes we'll need for a decent third act in the new normal of financial insecurity.

It is the book to read to help you navigate the emotional aspects of where you have landed. So many of you have told me how hard it is to get motivated for the future—and how down you feel. So let's pop the hood and take a look around.

55, Underemployed, and Faking Normal is where to turn when you feel that you're circling the drain and want to know what steps you can take to help gather and steady yourself enough to do what you need to do to go the next round.

The book takes a crack at two of the three big nuts that have a lot to do with our sense of well-being: where we live and our ability to supplement our incomes in our later years.[7]

Housing is often one of the biggest nuts we have to crack. As one boomer-aged friend said, "If I have housing, I can 'extreme coupon' it the rest of the way." Solving the housing problem lifts a boulder off our backs.

Income is the other big one. Many of us will be working much longer than we ever imagined—well into our seventies and even beyond. We find ourselves suddenly in the workforce after divorce or the illness or death of a spouse. Others of us have jumped or been pushed out of our jobs and are trying to figure out what's next.

We dread ending up as greeters at Walmart or, possibly worse, as the resident dinosaur in offices where our supervisors are the same age as our youngest children.

For many of us, work in the new-normal world can and will look different than it did in the past. Think freelance, multiple income streams, or working from home. Fewer and fewer of us will be sitting all day with our feet under someone else's desk.

This book aims to help us navigate these waters and learn from our contemporaries who are doing so successfully.

We don't have the same options we used to have. As my friend Robert says, "We're in the midst of a seismic shift. The paradigms that used to serve us no longer do." To see what works, we are going to have to consider all the levers at our disposal.

I lost everything. A stress-related health crisis and a bankruptcy later, I was destitute and needed to "get back out there." The job market has passed me by. I stayed on my throne, though, scoffing at the idea of seeking lower-level work and figuring that I could just think and muscle and network my way back to "having it all." It has been difficult to realize that the days of me winning by society's standards are probably over. It has been tough knowing that peers and family don't quite understand why I don't "start a business" or "get into real estate" or the like. It is demoralizing when the only replies to your résumé are from people who want you to sell your products for no base pay or benefits. Many of my peers are winding down and my mentors are out of the game, which makes networking challenging. I put on a happy face and fight back feelings of worthlessness. I struggle not to hate myself for ending up like this after all the work of a lifetime.

—Ralph

How This Book Is Organized

Let's look back before we go forward. And, on this score, we can learn something from an elderly black woman I know as "Auntie." Although the life lessons she can offer us hark back to simpler times, there's still much that we can learn from them today. You don't have to take the whole "bouquet" of advice: Just pluck what's relevant for you.

Then let's look at how we got into this situation in the first place. The specific details are different in each case, but there are some systemic issues beyond individual behavior that landed millions and millions of boomer-aged Americans here. This investigation will give you context and hopefully help you stop blaming and beating up on yourself.

We have tough choices to make ahead. To regain mastery over our lives will require personal agency. We can't be proactive if we're depressed, guilt-ridden, hiding with the covers over our heads, and wasting valuable energy pretending we're fine.

So once we understand how we got here, we will deal with our mind-sets and attitudes. Because if our heads are out of whack—if we're in denial, in a rut, and turned inward—nothing will get through to us. We'll just be going through the motions and looking without seeing. In that state we'll be sure to miss any good opportunities that might come our way.

We look outward at our options too. What can we really expect when we're living on modest incomes? Most of us are going to have to work longer for less money than what we're used to making. How do we wrap our brains around that and make peace with it—flourish, even?

Resilience Circles

When I lost my job three years ago, one friend in particular proved to be my touchstone and sanity refuge. Like me, she was a former high earner dealing with a major work gap and an unstable income. We were brutally honest with each other. We used to play this crazy game called "Top This" to get relief from the stress. I would share that my cell phone was about to be disconnected for nonpayment. She would counter that her water had been turned off. It was the crisis sweepstakes. The person with the worst situation won. I know, I know, it sounds morbid, but in some of the worst moments it made all the difference. Our friendship was one of very few places I could go without feeling I had to "fake normal," or pretend I was all right.

We talked about other things, too, like who we were without our props and credentials and our "job identities." We talked about what had meaning for us now at this age and stage when so much had been stripped away. We talked about what we wanted to take into the future and what we wanted to leave behind. We mirrored back to each other the people we'd been before we'd experienced such economic turmoil. This friend, a few others, and my mother and daughter were the barriers between the abyss and me. I was still broke, but how I held being broke had changed. And that allowed me to take my first steps back from the abyss.

That's why I suggest that you read this book with other faking-normal travelers in what I'm calling a "Resilience Circle," or RC. And I strongly urge you to do so if you feel that you're circling the drain, exhausted by the sheer effort it takes to pretend you're fine when you're not. For me, finding my tribe and being part of a supportive community is critical to my sense of well-being and key to my ability to choose what's right for me and to act on my own behalf. And I believe it could be for you too.

Creating Your Resilience Circle

You likely already know one person among your friends and friendly acquaintances who is faking it, and that person likely knows one other, and so on. That's enough to begin.

Approach that person. Tell him or her that you'd like to start a small group: a Resilience Circle to support each other and to discuss issues related to aging and living a good life on a limited income. Along the way, you will utilize many resources, but this book is designed to get you started.

Hold meetings even if your Resilience Circle consists of just you and two or three other people at the beginning. It's hard to navigate these waters alone. Isolation is crazy making. Peer-to-peer support can keep you even-keeled and open to possibility.

Keep the logistics simple. Meet in someone's home or in the library. Make it cheap. Don't go overboard with the refreshments—or serve no food or drinks at all.

But, you say, you don't really have any friends, or, none who live near you. And you can't picture yourself starting a group with strangers—never done anything like that before. How do you get one of these Resilience Circles going in this case?

Your public library is a good resource. Libraries have changed a lot since when we were growing up. Many have morphed into full-fledged community centers with wide ranging programming and events, including book clubs. So, why not enlist your local library's help in starting a Resilience Circle? They can even order the books.

Same with churches—many have programs that teach debt elimination, money management, financial literacy, and accountability, all themes consistent with *55, Underemployed, and Faking Normal*. Your church, then, might be another place you could go for help starting your Resilience Circle.

What if your "fake" is so good that no one knows your situation? Well, are you on Facebook or LinkedIn? Post "You Know Her," the essay included in the beginning of this book, on social media. Ask who would like to meet to discuss this and other issues related to aging and "rewiring" for the fourth quarter.

When "You Know Her" was published on PBS's Facebook page, it received 11,000 "likes" in three days. I guarantee that you will get a big response. Your challenge will be having too many people, not too few.

It would be great to meet in person, but if you don't live near the folks you have connected with, why not talk on the phone?

Also, don't make the group too big. Your group is your safe place. It's where you get to open your kimono and say what is true for you. You will be sharing personal information. You don't need a cast of thousands for that. Between four and six people is probably enough.

I like the idea of mixed-gender groups, but you can decide what works for you.

You will figure out how you want to structure your group, how often you want to meet, what you want to focus on, and other ground rules.

Initially, the topics you discuss will follow the chapters in *55,*

Underemployed, and Faking Normal, but as the Resilience Circle progresses, the topics you discuss will depend entirely on your circle's interests and priorities.

Depending on how often your RC meets, this book will get you through the first three or four months.

I've included some questions to get you started at the end of each chapter. Of course, you will also come up with questions and resources of your own.

There's one last thing: Why not start your meeting with the "Top This" sweepstakes? I know, I know . . . it's corny!

Do it anyway.

Each person should write a few sentences on a page and put it in a bowl. No names. Someone read each "Top This" entry aloud.

When folks have been faking it for a long time, it becomes second nature. The "Top This" sweepstakes quickly gets people past self-puffery to *Wow . . . there are a lot of people in this boat with me.* It keeps your RC 100 percent honest.

Every eight seconds, another American turns sixty-five; that's some 10,000 people per day. By 2030, nearly 20 percent of the population will be sixty-five or older, comprising the largest senior population in the history of the United States. And millions of boomer households are financially unprepared: one extended health crisis, job loss, or traumatic event from insolvency.

This reality, while well known to experts working on senior issues, is largely missing from political and public discourse. As individuals facing this situation, we've got to start talking about it if we want to find solutions. This book, in conjunction with the Resilience Circles that it proposes, is a place to start. We're going to have to use our strength in numbers to change the national la-la land conversation on retirement income security. And we're going to have to sound the alarm and push our institutions and public-policy makers to go hard on this crisis with the urgency it deserves.

Getting Started

♦ This first Resilience Circle gathering is really about meeting one another if you are not already friends and addressing some of the logistics and procedural questions. Where do you want to meet, how often, duration of meetings, etc.? And then there are those of you who might be meeting remotely and figuring out how that will work— i.e., whether you'll talk on the phone, over Skype, using FaceTime, or via some other service.

♦ As part of your logistics discussion, you'll also want to talk about how you'll end your time together. Will your RC be over when you finish this book? Or is 55, Underemployed, and Faking Normal just a starting place? You may not be able to answer this question now, but do revisit it later so that the closeout is orderly, not abrupt, and honors the work you've done together.

♦ Think of Resilience Circles as convening places where you can learn from one another and share information about helpful resources related to living more secure, connected, rich, and textured lives as you age.

♦ You will want to invite each person in your Resilience Circle to commit to coming to the meetings and working through the book. Intentions matter. We're talking about holding meetings for three or four months, depending on how often you meet. Obviously, life happens, so make sure that your group is big enough to deal with the inevitable absences and natural attrition.

♦ You will want to appoint a group leader or moderator to keep the discussions on track. Maybe this can be a rotating position so that no one person is overly burdened.

♦ You will likely not get through each chapter's reflection questions in a single meeting. Take two or three meetings if you need to; it's not a race or a contest. Work through all of the questions as best you can and see where they take you and what they spark in you.

◆ You'll also want to affirm the importance of confidentiality. Typically, we don't show up to gatherings like this; instead, we bring our faking-normal representatives—the parts of ourselves that appear to fit in and pretend to be all right. If we've been faking it for a long time, we've gotten good at it, with carefully cultivated stories and personas. Your Resilience Circle is your safe place to drop all of that. It's where you get to do some honest processing and problem solving with peers. That's why confidentiality is so important.

◆ Your Resilience Circle is not your therapy session, though. Sometimes, when we haven't candidly shared our experiences in a long time, we are full to the brim. We have so much to say. It's easy to get wrapped up in our stories and to go on and on and on. In part, this is a time-management issue, and your RC will want to agree on some guidelines. But you will also want to reflect on your readiness to join a Resilience Circle. Is it too early? Are you in such a dark place, so angry, or in such a downward spiral that what you really need is counseling—or counseling in parallel with the Resilience Circle? You may not know the answer to that yet. Sometimes we can be in denial about what's going on with us even though our pain is clear to others.

◆ Consider starting each meeting with three minutes—three full minutes—of silence. Keep your eyes open and really look at who is in the room with you. A lot of us come into this process pretty banged up. Reestablishing these simple human connections can help us make the changes that we need to make to shape better futures. In the beginning it will feel uncomfortable and awkward to not fill the silence with chatter. Do it anyway. Consider it an "Elizabeth-ism." I ask you to trust me on this one. It's powerful. Drop me a line. I'd like to know what you experience.

◆ And of course, I encourage you to do the "Top This" exercise that I described in the introduction. You could have everyone submit their anonymous entries on pieces of paper and then have the group decide on a winner. I suspect that you'll drop the anonymity fairly quickly and speak the truth to one another directly.

Chapter 2

Old-school Wisdom from an Elderly Black Woman

One one coco full a basket.

—Jamaican proverb

I want to take us back before I take us forward and tell you about my mother's cousin Anne, whom I knew as "Auntie." Auntie is gone now; she died some years ago at the age of eighty-three. Auntie was colorful, and not every aspect of her story will speak to you. But when you look beyond her eccentricity to the simple principles that guided her life, you will find much in this old black woman's experience that will help us navigate the road ahead.

Auntie spent holidays with my family. Homemade Christmas eggnog was her specialty, with enough bourbon in it to cross your eyes.

She was a short, round woman, and her weight caused her to sway gently from side to side as she walked. To steady herself, she trailed her fingertips along the wall and across countertops.

Auntie loved Jesus and her church.

At home she wore white gloves in the New York City summer heat. Her knees showed above her rolled-down stockings and orthopedic shoes.

She must have been quite a sight as she, cane in hand, made her way into the branch office of her local bank.

She was sweating and tired from taking the bus, and rested on a bench in the bank's lobby to catch her breath.

As she tells the story, one of the security guards saw her and asked her to move along. According to Auntie, he was polite at first but then insisted that she leave the premises.

Auntie didn't want to make a fuss, but this was her bank, after all, and she had a right to be there. She asked to speak with the manager.

He finally came out and spoke to Auntie in hushed tones. He apologized, of course, but did not protest when Auntie, still stung by how she'd been treated, declared that she'd be taking her business elsewhere.

The bank manager stood next to her as she gave the teller her account number. Distracted, he was barely listening when she asked for her account balance.

Auntie, with pursed lips and her hand resting on her cane, slid the paper over to him. He glanced down and then away, trying to mask his surprise at all those zeros in Auntie's six-figure balance.

Auntie said he was scrambling now. This old black woman who minutes before had been mistaken for a bag lady was suddenly a fine, upstanding member of the community.

Auntie worked as a private-duty nurse and never made more than $30,000 in any given year. Yet, even after paying tithes, she left behind the largest estate of any member of my family. Today her Fort Greene brownstone alone is valued at $3.7 million.

Auntie never sipped a latte, worked out with a personal trainer, or spent the equivalent of a car note on a pair of shoes.

She bought her brownstone in the mid-1950s as a young woman fresh off her family's farm in Kentucky. To make ends meet, she rented rooms to boarders and, as she got up in age, looked for tenants who could also help with errands and home repairs.

Auntie never married but wore a wedding band. I'm not sure why; maybe for respectability in an era when childless, never-married women were labeled spinsters and old maids. She didn't take much stock in men. Laughing, she'd say they just "wear you down."

As children, we complained about how scratchy and stiff Auntie's towels were. She didn't believe in dryers and hung towels out to dry on the clothesline behind her house.

Once a month Auntie treated herself to a meal at Junior's on Flatbush Avenue. She saved the receipts and always rounded up to the next dollar to "leave a little something" for a tip.

Auntie loved playing the piano, although her feet barely touched the pedals of the upright sitting in her living room. But that did not stop her from belting out the church hymns she loved.

She thought pantyhose were a good invention. She kept them balled up in a basket near her bed. Most were missing one leg or the other, which Auntie cut off when it got a run in it: no need to throw away the whole thing, she said, when you could double up the "good" legs and wear them together.

Smooth talkers were always trying to get Auntie to sell her house. They offered the kind of money you'd think would impress someone of modest means, but it didn't work on Auntie. She knew the value of what she had and wanted no part of the cash windfall these men were peddling.

Auntie was eighty-three when she died in 2004. I believe she was satisfied with how her life had turned out and felt at peace. She had God, her church, her community, her family, and her music.

I think about Auntie and wonder what we might learn from the old-school values that shaped her life. What about the way she lived could serve us now? What values could help us navigate the rough retirement-security waters ahead?

Marketers could not lure her with shiny gadgets and new toys. She eschewed consumer demands that were completely manufactured and instead found her joy in simple, affordable pleasures.

She didn't talk about a sustainable economy. Nor did she use terms like *conservation, recycle,* or *repurpose.* She just saved all kinds of stuff and was never wasteful.

Friends and family were her security. Her network was her net worth. She valued people, and it showed in her actions. Years of living alone made Auntie a little eccentric and quirky, but she made time for us, and I could always feel the love and connection we shared.

We live in an era when most people would prefer to send an e-card than lick a stamp or pay someone a visit. A friend whose husband died recently lamented that she'd received few visitors and not a single honey-baked ham or lemon pound cake but lots of phone calls and texts.

There was no social media when Auntie was alive. I doubt that she would have approved of technology that gives you credit for "staying in touch" without investing the face time it takes to nurture family or to be a real friend.

Auntie was frugal and understood that every little bit adds up. The way she lived her life reminds me of the Jamaican proverb "One one coco full a basket," which roughly means that adding one coco root at a time will fill a basket. It speaks to being patient, working hard, and persevering. Don't try to do everything at once. Little efforts done consistently can get us to where we want to go.

And where Auntie was trying to go was to have enough to take care of herself and leave "a little something" for her family. And that she did.

Resilience Circle Reflection

Revisiting What Is Essential

Remember to do the "Top This" exercise and to start with three minutes of silence.

Auntie was clear about what she needed in order to have a rich and tex-tured life. She had God, church, community, family, and music. What do you need? What is essential to your happiness now? Try to push beyond your habitual responses and beyond the answers that you've given for so long that you don't even know whether they're true anymore.

* If we in your circle look at your life now, would we know what you value by the choices you're making? Does how you spend your money and time align with who you say you are and what you say matters to you?

* Although Auntie was not a wealthy woman, she was not tempted by smooth talkers offering fast cash for her biggest asset. Nor was she lured by the latest and greatest shiny new objects. She saved stuff and kept things until they fell apart. In a culture that beckons us to buy things to experience the emotions we desire—like buying a Hummer to feel powerful, to give an extreme example—how do you cut back without feeling deprived?

* Auntie did what she had to do to make ends meet, including taking in boarders. What actions are you resisting that you should be consid-ering? What's holding you back? For example, should you be moving out of the family home into a smaller place, getting rid of the contents of your storage unit, or taking that job that pays less—much less—than what you're used to making? Is there a way to look at these decisions as just strategies without taking on the failure label?

* What do we leave our children and grandchildren if we're not leaving them money? What's the price tag on a habitable planet, clean air, and safe drinking water? What is our role in making sure that these things are passed on?

Chapter 3

Shock and Awe:
You Call This Retirement?

This is not just women. My life is nothing like what I thought it would be, and I am so tired of pretending that everything is OK. I went from the top to the bottom, and it seems that nobody cares or wants to help.

—Bob

Let's go beyond the self-blame and all of the wouldas, couldas, and shouldas, and look at the systemic factors that have left tens of millions of older Americans financially vulnerable and insecure.

Scrimping and Scraping in Our Fifties and Sixties

None of us expected to be here: broke or nearly broke, unemployed or underemployed, or working part-time jobs we hate with little to nothing in our savings accounts.

We grew up thinking that retirement meant Florida and golf, not that most of us really wanted that. It definitely did not mean living in our brother's basement or in some modest one-bedroom rental. We never thought that in our fifties and sixties we'd be scrimping and scraping or borrowing money from our adult children or eighty-four-year-old mothers.

And yet here we are . . . millions of us, and millions more on the way.

I thought that I would be in a better place financially at fifty-nine, but, sadly, I am not. Life is just difficult. It is such a struggle financially, emotionally, and physically.

—Suzanne

My four kids asked me what I had for retirement, and I told them you.

—Pamela

And how big is the deficit between what Americans have and what they need to retire? According to the nonpartisan Employee Benefit Research Institute, EBRI, the deficit between what Americans have and what we need to retire is $4.13 trillion.[1]

Wrap your brain around that number. It assumes that we will be spending down *all* of our assets, including our home equity.

Consider the following facts: according to the most recent Federal Reserve Board/Department of Treasury Survey of Consumer Finances (released in September 2017), 35 percent of all American households hold no retirement accounts at all.[2] That's zero—no IRA or Keogh account, no 401(k), nada.

Even among those who do have retirement savings, the median account balance across all ages is paltry, totaling only $1,100.

You're thinking, maybe that's because near retirees have fat pensions stashed away somewhere. You'd be wrong. According to a 2017 Federal Reserve Report on the Economic Well-Being of U.S. Households, 26 percent of households aged fifty and above have neither retirement savings nor pensions.[3] That number swells to 44 percent when you include Gen Xers age forty and up.

And according to the Fed study, among those pre-retirees between fifty-six and sixty-one who do have some retirement savings, the median value of retirement accounts is $25,000.

I stopped mid-mascara when I heard that.

Even when you add in the average monthly social security benefit of $1,404, it's still depressing. And you're definitely screwed if you live in a major metropolitan area, where one-room studios go for that much. In fact, according to analysis by the *Wall Street Journal*, "40 percent of households headed by people aged fifty-five through seventy lack sufficient resources to maintain their living standard in retirement."[4]

So, What Happened?

I have close relatives in the same exact situation: well educated, worldly, used to be paid well till the bust of '08. It's been hard for them to come back. It was a harsh wake-up call for me to know that ageism still takes place and we, the young, are on the fast track to the same predicament.

—Mike

There's a lot of hand-wringing about why Americans aren't saving more. Blaming and shaming others is so deliciously tempting. We're told that it's our fault that, after working for our whole lives, we have not managed to save the fifteen to twenty times our annual salaries financial experts tell us we'll need to maintain our current standard of living in retirement.

The same pundits finger wag and chastise us for being poor planners. After all, why on earth would we draw from our 401(k)s to cover medical expenses, the monthly shortfalls in our mothers' nursing home care expenses, our kids' education, or just to survive? What were we thinking when we paid off that credit card debt? (You fill in the blank.)

Sadly, many of us don't even wait for strangers to blame and shame us: we are too busy beating up on ourselves.

I am hovering at the edge. And it is terrifying and embarrassing and terribly sad after a lifetime of hard work. I feel like I am the only one of my friends and family in this situation, though surely I can't be the only one. Some days it is hard not to feel like a loser.

—Frank

OK, so let's own our part. Over forty years we have made some financial mistakes and blunders and done some dumb stuff. And there is no denying that we all woulda, coulda, shoulda saved more if we hadn't bought X, Y, or Z.

But let's also get real. Excessive spending is not what landed millions of Americans here. The truth is that, for many households, there's just nothing left to save after the bills have been paid.

According to the Social Security Administration,[5] in 2016 (latest figures available) the average US worker's pay was $46,640. If we set aside in savings the 20 percent that financial experts tell us we'll need to maintain our current lifestyle in retirement, we'd be left with $37,312 to live on before taxes.

You might say that's hard but not impossible with some extreme belt tightening.

But here is the kicker: 67 percent of American workers make less than the average.[6]

The median wage in the United States in 2016 was $30,533, meaning that half made more and half made less than that. Set 20 percent, or $6,106, aside for savings, and you'd have $24,427 to live on.

FUGEDDABOUTIT. You're not going to save on those wages.

Those wages barely keep you above the federal poverty line of $20,780 for a family of three, and you fall below the poverty line for a family of four, which is $25,100.[7]

I am now earning two-thirds of what I earned two years ago, and that was by no means extravagant. After forty-five years in the workplace, I'll get a raise if the minimum wage goes up to fifteen dollars.

—Audrey

And we're not talking about some tiny number of American families who can't afford to pay their bills. In fact, 34.7 million households fall into this category. Researchers have even coined a name for them: ALICE: Asset Limited, Income Constrained, Employed.[8] That's a fancy way of describing people who are working hard, maybe even more than one job, but still can't afford to cover their basic needs for things like food, housing, transportation, and child care.

> *I am a nurse's assistant, forty-nine with a fourteen-year-old daughter. We are currently staying in my niece's bedroom. My sister and I used to get along really well, but now it's a lot of cold shoulders on her part and avoidance and isolation on mine.*
>
> —Charlotte

> *I am over fifty with a bachelor's degree, and since losing my best job in 2007, I have not had steady work. No 401(k) and couldn't send kids to college because of other financial problems. I can't afford to go back myself and have had ageism problems show up repeatedly to acquire a new job. We should become a political PAC on this.*
>
> —Lillian

The ALICE project analyzes county-level data by state and thus goes beyond traditional measures of poverty, which rely on national averages that many researchers maintain grossly underestimate the real number of people in financial jeopardy. In total, some 51 million households in the United States (43 percent of the total) have incomes below the ALICE threshold and the poverty line. Given this reality, no one should be surprised that more than half of Americans have less than $1,000 in their checking and savings accounts.[9] And according to a 2018 Federal Reserve Board study, 40 percent of us can't even pull together $400 to deal with an emergency.[10] This is paycheck-to-paycheck living with many people just one surprise event from financial catastrophe.

But, you say, what about all these glowing economic headlines? Isn't the unemployment rate dropping month after month? True. It's all true. It's just not the only thing that's true. We get misled when we don't look at the whole board. We start thinking things are rosier than they are, that we're the only ones grinding it out financially, struggling to make ends meet.

There was a lot of fanfare when the Bureau of Labor Statistics (BLS) reported a 4 percent unemployment rate in July 2018. What got much less attention was the 7.8 percent *underemployment rate* which includes discouraged job seekers who have given up looking for work and part-time workers who'd prefer to work full-time.[11]

In other words, that 4 percent unemployment rate does not include the long-term unemployed, the folks who, after putting in hundreds of job applications, just give up on ever finding work. It also doesn't include all the people working part-time who want to work full-time, folks working beneath their skill level in precarious low wage jobs, barely scraping it together on fifteen-, twenty-, twenty-five-hour work weeks.

That's why many economists consider 7.8 percent, known as the U-6 rate, to be a more comprehensive and accurate measure of unemployment because it covers the percentage of the labor force that is unemployed, underemployed, and discouraged.

We can also look at the official July 2018 unemployment rate for people over fifty-five, our cohort. It's a rosy 3.1 percent. Again, this statistic does not include discouraged workers. BLS defines discouraged workers as workers "who have looked for work sometime in the past twelve months . . . but are not currently looking because they believe there are no jobs available or there are none for which they would qualify."[12]

That one-year limit is arbitrary. If you stopped looking one year and one day ago you're not counted. We all know people our age who want to work, need to work, but haven't looked in over a year, beat down and shell-shocked by one job rejection after another. The official 3.1 percent unemployment rate does not include them. According to SCEPA's Retirement Equity Lab (ReLab), there are 1.1

million older adults "who reported last month that they want a job but have not looked in the last year."[13] Based on ReLab calculations when they are added, the total unemployment rate for workers over fifty-five jumps to 7.3 percent.

And sure, you might be employed, but in what kind of job? According to ALICE project data, "two-thirds of the jobs in the US pay less than twenty dollars per hour." And don't be fooled when some talking head tells you that the number of jobs held by older workers has increased by 6.6 million over the last decade. What they won't tell you is that over half of those jobs—52 percent or over 3.4 million—paid full-time workers less than $15,000 per annum.[14]

And You're No Deadbeat

Here's a sobering truth: many of us who have worked fifty or more years find ourselves in this terrifying situation. At sixty-six, I am unexpectedly unemployed and identify with these feelings. That was not the plan. I am trying not to panic as I identify puzzle pieces, put them firmly together, and ride the roller coaster of emotions. I could live another thirty or more years. I'll do whatever I can and hope that my safety net remains firmly in place.

—Sydney

Millions and millions of Americans did not end up here because of profligate spending. According to Teresa Ghilarducci, a labor economist and leading authority on the economics of retirement, the looming retirement income crisis is not caused by "a set of isolated individual behaviors."[15]

In other words, you're not here because you're a deadbeat. And you're not here because you overspent on luxury items trying to keep up with the Joneses.

HelloWallet,[16] an innovative online investment and savings service, conducted a survey in 2013 to find out why one in four Americans dip into their 401(k) accounts before they reach retirement age. This "leakage" in the form of withdrawals, cashouts, and loans accounts for $70 billion, or nearly a quarter of the $293 billion that workers and employers deposit into their accounts annually.

What HelloWallet researchers found is that three-quarters of the people raiding their retirement savings are using the money to pay mortgages, rent, and medical bills; to make car repairs; and so on. In other words, for the most part, these withdrawals are not for discretionary spending.

Squeezed between flat wages and rising expenses, millions of Americans feel as though they have no choice but to tap into their 401(k) accounts just to make ends meet.

And being retired gets harder every year. Believe me, with insurance and health-care expenses skyrocketing, especially pharmacy, it is harder and harder to get along on a fixed income.

—Neil

The truth is, if you're a boomer-age American, you've spent your last three or more decades dealing with flat or falling wages, disappearing pensions, and steeply rising costs in housing, health care, and education. As if that pummeling weren't bad enough, in 2008 you were hit by the largest economic downturn in decades.

And for older Americans in our fifties, sixties, and beyond, recessions are especially bad news because we no longer have the time to make up losses. At this stage we're looking more to returns than to new contributions to build our retirement nest eggs. And returns can take time that we don't have.

Lattes, Bottled Water, and Other Myths

I always thought there would be another job or more clients or something, but to have to admit we made poor money choices and career decisions and ended up on the slag heap, unwanted and unvalued. I'm still bewildered and ashamed and at a loss

for a way to explain it to myself without making excuses . . .
I've made mistakes, but with my skills and experience. I de-
serve better than this.

—Cynthia

You are going to hear a lot about how it's all your fault that you underfunded your retirement; you'll hear about all of that money you wasted on lattes and bottled water. You're going to be accused of being irresponsible and fiscally promiscuous—yes, promiscuous.
Don't buy it.
According to finance guru Helaine Olen, the costs of coffee and other small, meaningless luxuries don't hold a candle to the escalating costs of health care, housing, and education.[17]
In other words, it's doubtful that kicking your daily latte habit—if you had one—would have made much of a difference in your retirement savings.
Olen said that she would have to forgo 520 coffee drinks per month just to cover her monthly health insurance bill.[18] In other words, you are not going broke because of your trips to Starbucks.
So let's own our roles in underfunding our retirement but reject this nonsense that what has happened to us is mainly due to our personal irresponsibility, wastefulness, and frivolous buying. For the overwhelming majority, the financial beatings we're taking as we enter our fifties, sixties, and beyond have been mainly outside of our control.

I am in the same boat: MBA, broke, living in my son's base-
ment, hiding for the most part while most of my online appli-
cations disappear. I've finally taken a job at Home Depot and
start tomorrow. I'm hungry and only go up and take food when
no [one] is around, because even family members feel resentful
when you end up like this. Only I don't want to end up like this.
I want to feel good again.

—Martin

Meet Bruce

This is Bruce's story in his own words:

It was the quiet that bothered me the most. That and the season changes reminded me that I was standing still while the snowflakes fell and the leaves died and came back again.

Believe me, that hurt, deep and long.

My career trajectory went along with risks and rewards and my continued push for an engaged and engaging sense of self. As a kid from Brooklyn, with working-class parents and the first generation to graduate from college, I had come a long way from my days behind the wheel of a cab. That was tough, working overnights and driving back and forth through the deadly New York streets to simply earn enough to pay the rent, and only to get up and do it again the next day.

But I was determined and got lucky after having had to drop out of journalism grad school because I simply couldn't afford it. Somehow I stumbled, worked, and risked my way through jobs at NPR stations in North Carolina and Wisconsin and ended up in this new little outfit just starting out of the old Jewish Men's Club of Atlanta. It was called CNN. Then I hustled to New York, did freelance gigs with the networks, and had a twenty-five-year-long career with NBC, CBS, ABC, and ESPN.

My life and experiences seemed to move in lockstep as a writer and producer, heading from covering the Olympics, wars, and campaigns to doing top assignments on the *Today* show, *Nightly News, Dateline, Good Morning America*, and the like. Gumbel, Brokaw, Williams, and dozens of others read what I wrote and produced winning contracts and accolades along the way. This was a rough trade. It took work and a stiff constitution to cut through the political crap and just be an honest guy telling an honest tale. And then things changed.

First, I got older. Next, infotainment and younger regimes moved in at an ever-quickening pace. My assignments got weaker, the budgets got smaller, and I went from an office to a cubicle and then to a part-time space, and then out in a matter of years. I looked around and I was in my mid-fifties. And suddenly my phone, which used to be answered at the White House and in the halls of Congress, was dead silent at home.

I had been downsized into oblivion.

Now, some will argue, of course, that we all are masters of our own fates and the captains of our own ships, which was the credo I had followed on my successful voyage. Still, the same risk-taking, frontline style that had made for a remarkable career was dead. We old-timers held on like polar bears to shrinking ice ridges while younger, cheaper Ivy Leaguers pushed through with blind ambition and nary a thought for my blood or the blood of others on the side of the road.

At fifty-five, I was home, unemployed, and knee-deep in the 2008 recession. I had little hope of grabbing a life ring in the new digital economy.

Oh, I tried. Believe you me, I tried. Indeed, I wasn't alone— thank God. Correspondents I'd traveled with to war zones and elsewhere were also on the over-fifty-five scrap heap. I'd talk to some every day as we sought out sanity and voices of support in a silent world that didn't know or care about our stories, our pasts, our accomplishments, or our awards. We had become invisible—except, of course, to the bill collectors and to relatives and friends.

That was the worst rub, I guess. People who knew me all had the same reactions, like: "What did that asshole say to get himself blacklisted?" or "All you have to do is reinvent yourself."

That was the worst—the absolute worst. They didn't seem to understand what it was like to send out hundreds and thousands of résumés and to get no personal responses. They didn't understand that somehow you could become trapped in a vortex of being unwanted and out of step no matter how many skills you tried to update, how many pounds you tried to lose, how many new sport coats you bought, or how many different options you pursued. All you had to do, they said, was "reinvent yourself." It was simple.

Lord knows, I tried. My meetings with business and career psychologists and coaches and résumé writers, my parallel-career interviews with folks in PR, and my attempts to start a business marketing nonfiction television were met with amused stares. There were no responses from the nonprofits we had supported financially and otherwise. In the end I remember chucking six lawn-and-leaf garbage bags full of letters, notebooks, résumés, and outreaches for jobs and positions that I thought might kick-start my career after decades of deadline-driven, high-profile, high-paying work.

The hardest thing is understanding that you're still the same person who was successful, with the same drive and the same mind and the same-quality work ethic that allowed you to succeed and achieve at the highest levels. You know what it's like to work on no sleep, to meet your deadlines, to talk to people from every background, and to show up on time, prepared, and ready to lead, engage with others, and create and produce.

But now it worked against you. I was up at six in the morning at my computer, ready to rock by eight, and there was nowhere to go and no one left to call. Those in the biz were hanging on and happy to be working amid the fear of their own demises. You suddenly realized that folks wanted to avoid you because they didn't want to become you. People who had shared in your riches and successes and goodwill now avoided you, didn't return your calls, or seemed not to know what to say when you got together.

It was another level of loss when all you needed was just a chance to be who you were—the same guy—over a burger and a beer.

This, of course, continued while I worked legions of lousy part-time jobs that amounted to mostly nothing. Some were marginalized, horrid pieces of busywork or part-time work for federal agencies or even adjunct teaching gigs where you're a fill-in with more work experience than most on the faculty and paid two grand for three courses for the semester.

Meanwhile, your income is dropping like a depth-charged, fatally damaged submarine racing uncontrollably to the bottom.

And then there's that other part: hanging on to yourself as the hours, days, and months merge into one, and then the seasons change. It's the conversations you are stuck with each day inside your head as you head out to the diner for a cup of coffee or a sandwich that you feel guilty about buying. Now you're the guy who's walking and talking to himself.

Amid the woes and the self-doubt, you might take some time to nap. But even that has its troubles, as sleeping can become a routinized part of your dysfunction and guilt. Even the conversations you have with yourself to reengage and restart are, in effect, false, because you know the score and have tried so many games only to end up in the same place the next day and every day after that.

It's hard not to corrode from the drops of water that tumble slowly and eat at the guts of your daily life. Frankly, lots of folks don't understand that success is sometimes simply surviving and recovering within yourself. I was lucky. While the drops fell, my wife still went to work and earned a good buck. I was lucky that, when my internal rage boiled over after shopping and cooking her dinner—my new job—she took it in stride. I was lucky that we'd put enough away for our kid to get his education. So damn lucky, yet I knew others who weren't.

At the end of the day, you're the same person. What sustained you for decades is who you are. You use that to reinvent yourself every day and to put up with the crap, satisfy what needs to be satisfied, and move on to do it again and again. Now I'm on the other side of this rainbow and accepting that luckily, I can retire. I'm damn lucky. But the scars are there, and the scar tissue is still new and fresh. The rage within and without from being trapped in a vortex of unemployment in a world of success is one dumb comment away from the surface.

I survived with the help of my family, a few close friends who never lost faith in me, and myself. Even with the good fortune of having food in the fridge, a damn good roof over my head, and friends and family who "get it," I wouldn't wish my pained years of being discarded by the digitized marketplace on a mean, rabid dog.

Here are some takeaways from what happened to me:

- Isolation and solitude can be deafening and devastating.

- It's rare to find friends and colleagues who truly understand your situation.

- Surviving rejection and rebuilding your inner self require inner strength and stamina.

- In the end, learn to be kind to yourself.

Resilience Circle Reflection

Looking Back So That We Can Move Forward

Remember to do the "Top This" exercise and to have three minutes of silence.

Too often, despite all of the discussions about the systemic factors that have contributed to the looming retirement crisis, we continue to make this crisis personal. We focus mainly on how we screwed up and on what we did wrong. We beat up on ourselves and put ourselves down. So, in this meeting, let's get it *all* out there so that we can move on and focus on what's ahead of us instead of on what's behind us.

- Let's talk about the wouldas, couldas, and shouldas. What two big things in your life do you wish you'd done differently? Let's keep our answers focused on actions that we feel negatively affected our finances. What do you know now that you didn't consider then? Give context without getting stuck in story or going into every last detail.

- When we think of our personal financial blunders, we think mainly about what they cost us. What about what we gained? For example, I depleted my savings when I invested in a retail business that was ultimately unsuccessful—but what an incredible ten-year ride it was. So, yes, I wish I had more coins in the bank, but, for the most part, I don't regret my foray into entrepreneurship and all that it taught me. And you? You know what your financial missteps cost you, but might there also have been upsides that you haven't considered?

- Are you still taking actions that negatively affect your finances—actions that you'd unreservedly put under the "personal irresponsibility" label? Let's get those out there too. We live in a culture that encourages us to buy things in order to feel the emotions that we want to feel. You know a particular action is financially irresponsible, but you're doing it anyway. Why? What need are you addressing?

- Too often when we're financially insecure and struggling daily with how to make ends meet, we engage in negative self-talk. What's your personal put-down of choice? What tape runs through your head (e.g., *loser* or *effing idiot*), that sort of thing? A friend once told me she felt like a "buffo-rilla." Let's get it all out there.

◆ This reflection is not a onetime event. You're not going to stop beating up on yourself after a single meeting. Today is just the start and a place to build. It's about knowing that you're not alone and that tens of millions of older Americans are facing their versions of your challenges.

Chapter 4

After a Lifetime of Work, How Did We Land Here?

I am fifty-nine and can't afford a car payment. I can't afford a higher rent or a mortgage. What I am saving won't make a dent in any retirement.

—Cate

As noted earlier, we hear a lot about how our retirement financial woes are all our fault because we lived beyond our means and spent all of our money trying to keep up with the Joneses. But that's not the main reason that tens of millions of older Americans have landed here, barely able to make ends meet.

The Wobbly Three-Legged Stool

The real problem is structural and baked into our retirement-security system. The three-legged stool of retirement income that we boomers thought we could count on—social security, company pensions, and personal savings—has gone wobbly. With the declining availability of employer-funded pensions; the inadequacy of 401(k) plans, with their steep fees and dependence on people voluntarily saving money for forty years and knowing how to invest wisely; the sharp drop in personal savings; and thirty-plus years of stagnant wages, many near retirees are left with what some experts describe as the "pogo stick" of social security during their golden years.

Things have changed dramatically since social security was first introduced back in 1935. Back then, the average twenty-one-year-old male had about a 50 percent chance of making it to the age of sixty-five. To put that in context, you retired at sixty, sat in your rocking chair, went fishing, kissed your grandkids, and died within five years of collecting benefits.

Today life expectancies can exceed eighty years, depending on race and gender—meaning that if you're a boomer in your early sixties and in good health, you're going to need enough income/savings to support you for the next two decades or more.

Social security was never intended to be *the* retirement plan. In the 1950s the promise was that it would provide a base of income for American workers, who would then supplement it with occupational pensions and personal savings.

But pensions are fast becoming a relic of the past, and with real wages flat or falling for decades, millions of boomer-aged Americans are too strapped to save and are struggling just to meet their basic expenses. They're entering their retirement years with only social security to depend on, with the average retiree receiving only $16,848 annually.

And many of you, especially women, have told me that you're surviving on a lot less than the average.

The future is unclear, with only my social security as my income. I'm learning to pinch pennies and to preserve what assets I have, but I find that my clothes are tattered.

—Mary

According to the Social Security Administration, in 2016, 64 percent of women and 56 percent of men elected to file for social security benefits early, at age sixty-two, which locked them into payments as much as 30 percent lower over their lifetimes than if they had waited until their full retirement age of sixty-six to file for benefits.

And we saw an increase in early filings during the 2008–2009 financial crisis as out-of-work older Americans applied for early social security benefits to replace their lost incomes.

I also lost my job in '09. Every job I applied for I was overqualified—and too old at sixty. After using up all of my extensions of unemployment, I was forced to take social security early and lost about $900 a month by doing so.

—John

Those who take early retirement are buying groceries, fully stalled in the job market. It really is a huge quagmire and the perfect storm: globalization (tanking wages) and automation (fewer needed) meet experienced baby boomers living twenty-five years longer than past generations.

—Sarah

Bag Lady Blues

For women sixty-five and older, the average monthly social security benefit is just $1,243.58[1] (versus $1,565.45 for men).[2] Without social security, nearly half of women sixty-five and older would be living in poverty or extreme poverty.

Let's get real here and define *extreme poverty*. It means living on less than $5,500 per year, or $458 per month.

This is my mom. I fear that if it weren't for her children, she would be homeless. Just as she was getting in a safe financial place, she suffered a stroke that has put her out of work for at least three months. She decided to take early social security, which has been a blessing and a curse. It's guaranteed income, but it's $500 for the rest of her life. I know all of this weighs on her constantly, *never giving her a chance at peace. She's the woman who gave me the world, and it is so hard to see her struggle.*

—Abigail

This is why the budget battles on Capitol Hill—which *threaten* to cut social security and other social insurance programs like Medicare and Medicaid—are so ludicrous. What we're really talking about is dooming millions and millions of boomer-aged women to misery and destitution.

We're not talking about some abstract group. We are talking about ourselves and about people we know: our sisters, our mothers, and our friends.

According to US Census Bureau data, many more women (4.4 million) than men (2.8 million) age sixty-five and older live in poverty.[3]

With fewer financial resources to fall back on, many women are filing for social security early. This shores women up in the short term, but, as noted earlier, taking early social security payments can reduce women's lifetime benefits by as much as 30 percent.

Dumped by my nonprofit charitable organization along with fifty-five other older employees, we had to sign that we wouldn't sue in order to get our six months of severance pay. Being sixty-three, I was never able to get a new job. I gave up after a year and applied for early social security payments.

—Sheila

With poverty rates for older women so much higher than those for men, it's no wonder that, according to one study,[4] half of US women fear becoming bag ladies.

I am a single woman who's sixty-five years old and will never be able to retire on the social security I receive. My consulting jobs have dried up, but fortunately, for now, I get paid by my daughter to babysit my one-year-old granddaughter. But what will happen when she goes off to school? What will happen to me? I, too, look at homeless women differently and wonder if I will be there someday. I look at my friends who are comfortably retired and find excuses not to socialize with them—even though I need to connect with others desperately—because I cannot afford to keep up with their lifestyles. Or I reluctantly accept friends' generous offers to pay restaurant checks and feel humiliated that my pockets are turned out.

—Wendy

Women Live Longer on Less

Women typically live longer than men and thus will need to fund longer retirements. In fact, today there are some 5.7 million more women age sixty-five and over than there are men.[5]

And that's not the only obstacle women face. There is, of course, the gender wage gap. According to the latest data from the US Census Bureau, the typical woman working a full-time, year-round job earned seventy-nine[6] cents for every one dollar that a man earned in 2016; Asian American women earned eighty-seven cents on the dollar, African American women earned sixty-two cents on the dollar, and Hispanic and Latina women earned fifty-four cents on the dollar.[7]

I have learned to live frugally. I only buy stuff when it's falling apart. I haven't seen a doctor in five years. Luxury for me now is being able to go to a restaurant and buy what I want to eat and not just what I can afford. It's being able to buy books again and to pay all my bills in the month they're due.

—Chris

On average, this wage-disparity gap costs a woman about $430,480 over a forty-year career. Lifetime-earning losses are even greater for African American and Latina women, costing them

$877,480 and $1,007,480, respectively.[8] Add to this shortfall another $324,044, which is the amount that women, as family caregivers, forfeit by taking time off from their paid work to tend to their parents,[9] and the hundreds of thousands more that they forfeit caring for children and other family members, and the consequences of spending a lifetime at an economic disadvantage become clear in lost wages and reduced pensions and social security benefits.

This is me at sixty, frugal, no job, no cable, no income. I spend my whole day in my tiny room wondering when my savings will run out.

—Annie

For all of these reasons, women nearing retirement are particularly disadvantaged. Millions face the risk, and increasingly the reality, of being old and poor in America. A recent study by the National Institute on Retirement Security on women's financial futures found that "women are 80 percent more likely than men to be impoverished at age 65 and older, while women between ages seventy-five and seventy-nine are three times more likely than men to be living in poverty."[10]

The prospect is worse if you are a woman of color who's sixty-five years old or older. According to the Sargent Shriver National Center on Poverty Law, "20.9 percent of black women, 19.6 percent of Hispanic women, 18.6 percent of Native American women, and 16.0 percent of Asian American women live in poverty, compared to 9.9 percent of white women."[11] And these numbers are rising.

I recently met a few of these women when I offered a room for rent. Talk about lost. They all worked hard, had children, lost husbands, and are now without income. What a loss.

—Thea

The Canary in the Coal Mine

Walking the streets of downtown San Francisco recently, I encountered whole blocks of homeless people side by side, standing, sitting, lying on flattened cardboard boxes, and in wheelchairs, walkers, and tents. There were men and women of every description and age, including older adults. Of course I have seen homeless people before, but not like this, not in a major city's high-rent district, not block after block after block. It was overwhelming.

I admit wanting to look away, to ignore what I was seeing by pretending to be on my phone. *The violence of looking away.* That thought kept running through my mind. It would be so easy to disengage, to look without seeing. I thought about all the stories behind those faces, all those eyes looking into mine.

I wondered if what I was seeing was just the tip of the iceberg, the proverbial canary in the coal mine, the pebbles before a landslide. Was it what we'd all soon be seeing in cities and towns across the country as our nation's retirement income crisis spills into the streets?

In their new book, *Rescuing Retirement: A Plan to Guarantee Retirement Security for All Americans,* labor economists Teresa Ghilarducci and Tony James tell us that "we will soon be facing rates of elder poverty unseen since the Great Depression," 20 million people by 2035. And in a report issued by the Schwartz Center for Economic Policy Analysis (SEPA), it's estimated that "40 percent of older workers and their spouses will be downwardly mobile, falling into poverty or near poverty in their old age."[12]

We won't have to read about these people on our newsfeeds. We will all know someone who has landed there, including those who were once part of the middle class. They will be our friends, our family members, ourselves.

Making It on the Pogo Stick of Social Security

Social security is the only leg of the three-legged stool that is holding somewhat steady. The others? Not so much.

Among private-sector workers with retirement plans, the percentage with only a pension has fallen from 62 percent in 1983 to 17 percent today. Over the same period, the percentage participating only in 401(k)-type plans increased from 12 percent to 73 percent.[13]

So basically we have gone from a retirement system that was automatic and managed for us by our employers to a voluntary, self-directed system where we have been given the reins and the risks. And it turns out that many of us just aren't that good at investing over the long term or trained or equipped to deal with market risks.

A Majority of Us Lack Basic Investment Expertise

How "in the dark" have we been?

A 2011 AARP survey found that seven in ten 401(k) participants did not know whether they were being charged fees.

According to a 2012 US Government Accountability Office (GAO) report, 80 percent of us had no idea what we were paying for in our 401(k) plans.

These findings are corroborated by a 2013 US Securities and Exchange Commission (SEC) study on financial literacy among retail investors mandated by the Dodd-Frank Wall Street Reform and Consumer Protection Act.

The Dodd-Frank report concluded that "investors have a weak grasp of elementary financial concepts and lack critical knowledge of ways to avoid investment fraud." It found that we don't know how to calculate fees, read account statements, identify basic financial products, or understand conflicts of interest.

And certain subgroups, such as women, African Americans, Hispanics, and the elderly, have lower levels of investment literacy than the general population.

In sum, at a time when we're expected to take on more and more responsibility for managing our retirement accounts, millions of us don't know how.

401(k)s: Do-it-yourself Pensions Are Failing Millions of Americans

Retirement remains a dream for most of us. We can't afford to retire or we'll lose our homes, which we've had to mortgage and refinance so that we could pay for our kids' education and medical bills (until Obamacare) and take care of our elderly relatives. Our pensions are small, our savings are ridiculously small, and our 401(k)s, a way to funnel savings to Wall Street firms.

—Christine

Remember all of that hype about how the terrific returns from our 401(k)s would replace pensions? Well, *that* didn't happen.

The great bull market of the 1980s and '90s masked serious defects in the 401(k)-type plans. When you're making double-digit returns, you don't worry much about fees. So, what if your broker made a percentage or two when the market was going up and up? It's a whole different story when the stock market tanks and your account balance is going down 30, 40, or 50 percent a year.

In this scenario, the shortcomings of the 401(k) savings model came into sharper focus. According to some experts, the most serious shortcoming is that it requires plan participants to manage their investments themselves.

Wall Street and politics are to blame. When they started pushing 401(k)s to replace defined benefit plans, they wanted the commissions.

—Mike

What You Have to Get Right to Manage Your 401(k) Plan Successfully

Planning for a secure retirement is much harder than planning for other big purchases, like, let's say, buying a home. Just think about everything you have to get right to manage your 401(k) plan successfully, and you'll see why our do-it-yourself pension system is failing millions of Americans.

You're expected to know what to invest in and to make consistently smart decisions over decades, managing your investments through stock market highs and lows with the right balance of stocks and bonds. Good luck with that!

You have to make assumptions about how long you will live, because if you die at eighty-seven, you'll need a lot more cash than if you die at sixty-seven.

You have to voluntarily save 10 percent—or, as some experts say, 15 to 20 percent—out of each paycheck for forty years despite flat wages and rising expenses.

You have to work out the financial impact of having children.

You have to know how much you will need for emergency savings and plan for Murphy's law to kick in, the loss of your job, a health-care crisis, and even death.

I won't torture you with the numbers, but let's take one quick example. Let's say you're a registered nurse in Illinois with a mean wage of $66,730. According to some financial experts, you would need to save *twenty times your annual salary, or $1,334,600*, in order to maintain your current standard of living in retirement. Really! A small percentage may be able to hit that target, but the truth is that it won't be happening for most people.

You have to resist tapping into your 401(k) savings for other purposes—like to pay for a health-care emergency, to build that deck on your home, or to pay your kids' college tuition.

And when you finally do retire, you have to know how much to draw from your savings. You'll want to take enough to live on but not so much that the well runs dry.

This is a steep hill to climb, and millions of Americans are not up to the task. The stats on 401(k) savings plans tell the whole story. In a study conducted by the National Institute on Retirement Security, using data from the US Federal Reserve, the median amount in 401(k) savings for all working households was $2,500, factoring in all those zeros for households with no savings at all. For near-retirement households age fifty-five to sixty-four, the median account balance was $14,500.[14]

With life expectancy rates now well into the eighties, there's no way any of us will survive on that.

Sure, there are some people who are very comfortable making retirement savings and investment decisions, and a few will hit it big, but that won't be the reality for most of us.

The Racial and Ethnic Divide in Retirement Security Widens

The decline in employer-sponsored pensions has also exacerbated certain racial and ethnic disparities in retirement readiness, leaving black and brown families among the least prepared for retirement.

Consider the following fact: according to the Corporation for Enterprise Development (CFED; now called Prosperity Now) 2016 Assets & Opportunity Scorecard,[15] black workers' rate of participation in employer-based retirement plans used to be similar to that of white workers, but black workers began lagging behind white workers in the 401(k) era, and Hispanic workers fell even further behind.

According to the Scorecard, "only 41 percent of black families and 26 percent of Latino families had retirement account savings in 2013 compared to 65 percent of whites." Furthermore, "even among families nearing retirement (age 56–61), the majority of black and Hispanic families have no retirement account savings."

And among those black and Latino families who did have savings in 2013, the median amount was $22,000, compared to $73,000 for white families.

Almost to the person, every black woman I know over fifty is facing a very precarious financial future. The only exceptions are the few who stuck it out in careers in government or the private sector. Married black women are better off, too, but a lot of black women have never been married.

—Juan

Add to this scenario one financial shock, job loss, or major repair to an appliance, and whatever money a family has saved will go toward dealing with the emergency, leaving that family even more vulnerable than before.

The inadequacy of 401(k) plans and the decline in employer-sponsored pensions are thus major causes of the retirement-income crisis—and black and brown households have been hit particularly hard by it.

New Federal Disclosure Rules Help, but Challenges Remain

In sum, most employees don't have the investment expertise to manage these 401(k)-type savings plans. They are in the dark about the returns they're getting on their assets, and fuzzy about their plans' fees and about the expenses they paid for participation.

Experts say that even today few employees inquire about the fees they are paying, despite federal disclosure requirements, the numerous class action suits challenging the fees, and the reports discussing the plans' shortcomings.[16]

According to a GAO survey conducted in 2014, half of the small and medium-sized employers who were asked about 401(k) expenses were in the dark about whether "they or their plan participants paid investment management fees." According to the GAO, the participants paid. They also didn't know what fees were being charged by administrators, investment advisors, or mutual funds.

The folly of basing our retirement-income-security system on voluntary personal savings for forty years could not be clearer, and now millions and millions of Americans are entering their so-called golden years with barely enough money to get by.

But signs of the coming retirement crisis were visible on other fronts as well.

The Commerce Department's Bureau of Economic Analysis (BEA) just updated the 2017 US household savings rate to 6.7 percent from the 3.4 percent previously reported. This, of course, is good news, but not good enough 6.7 percent is less than half of the 15 to 20 percent experts tell us we need to sock away to have a secure retirement.

And for the millions of American workers living paycheck to paycheck, nearly 80 percent by some estimates,[17] there's just nothing left to save after the bills are paid. If pensions are the first wobbly leg of the three-legged retirement income stool, savings are the second one.

Those of us in our fifties and sixties now ought to think about how much we'll actually need to sustain us over the next twenty-five to thirty years. Based on the 4 percent safe withdrawal rule many experts recommend, we'll need a million-dollar nest egg just to generate $40,000 in annual retirement income. Like that's gonna happen.

No Worries—I'll Just Break into My Home Equity Nest Egg

Many boomers are banking on the equity in their homes to fund their retirements—and, for some, breaking into the home equity nest egg makes sense. But this strategy won't work for everyone. For starters, some of us don't own our homes. According to U.S. Census Bureau data on home ownership rates, 75.4 percent of American households 55–64 own their homes, leaving a quarter who do not.[18]

Second, you need to have built up substantial equity and not pulled it all out with a home equity loan, a home equity line of credit (HELOC), or a cash-out refinance. And you have to live in a place where real estate prices held during the recession or rebounded in the "recovery."

And this hasn't happened everywhere. Just think about how far in the hole we were when the housing market crashed.

A September 16, 2012, *New York Times* editorial summarizing Moody's Analytics reported that the US housing market crash of 2007 "erased nearly $6 trillion in equity and left nearly 13 million people owing a total of $660 billion more on their mortgages than their homes were worth."[19]

And the housing recovery since the collapse has been uneven, with millions of homeowners still struggling to put it behind them. According to Zillow, the online real-estate database company, the number of individual homes losing value or upside down has declined steadily from what it was at the height of the housing crisis. Today at 9.1 percent, it is less than a third of what it was back then. But 9.1 percent is still 4.4 million homeowners who owe more on their homes than they're worth, and well above the 5 percent historical average.

Also, according to Zillow, "in many areas, even as home values rise overall, large numbers of individual homes themselves are actually losing value"[20] or underwater. This is the case in metro areas like Virginia Beach, Chicago, Baltimore, Cleveland, and St. Louis where 10 percent or more of mortgages are in negative equity.

Housing Recovery Leaves Many Black and Brown Families Behind

Race and ethnicity also factor into disproportionately high "underwater" rates. *Underwater America: How the So-Called Housing Re-*

covery Is Bypassing Many American Communities, a 2014 report by the Haas Institute for a Fair and Inclusive Society, found that in 64 percent of the 395 US zip codes with the highest concentrations of negative equity, African Americans and Latinos accounted for at least half of the residents.[21]

Similarly, in "71 of the 100 hardest hit cities, African Americans and Latinos accounted for at least 40 percent of the population."

And according to Zillow, five years into the housing recovery, homeowners in predominantly black and brown neighborhoods are still more likely to be underwater, 20 percent and 12 percent respectively, than mortgage holders in predominantly white neighborhoods (under 10 percent).[22]

Beyond Social Security as "the" Retirement Plan

Remember those days when you could just tighten your belt and wait for things to return to normal? Well, that's not the case anymore.

We Americans have smaller home equity nest eggs, barely there pensions, and much-diminished savings. Social security has become the default retirement plan for tens of millions of us. Economists debate how dependent we are on the benefit. Even by conservative estimates, about one-quarter of retirees receive 90 percent or more of their retirement income from social security. And this number is likely to go up as Gen Xers and the youngest baby boomers enter their retirement years without pensions.[23]

Even some affluent boomers who've had professional careers and comfortable lives are now looking at downward mobility.

Now that we no longer have the luxury of time to accumulate big retirement nest eggs, what are our options? What trade-offs must we make? What changes in our mind-sets and attitudes must we adopt? Will we ever be able to feel something other than this constant worry and nagging fear? Is attaining a modicum of peace still in the cards? Dare we even hope for joy or happiness?

After interviewing dozens of people and hearing from thousands more, I see a silver lining in the new normal. Nope, we're not getting our old lives filled with stuff and more stuff back. We're going to have to change and adapt in some ways that we won't like. And some of us won't go willingly.

But there are alternative paths. Some of our contemporaries in our same boat are making a go of it, and there's a lot that we can learn from their experiences.

Taking Stock

Remember to do the "Top This" exercise and to have three minutes of silence.

We can't know how much time we have left. We do know that the time ahead is shorter than the time behind us. At our age and stage, we know that there are few guarantees and that much is uncertain. But still we have choice. The question is: Will we exercise our power to choose?

◆ Who in your life knows what's really happening to you and the true nature of the financial challenges you're facing? How are you faking normal with the people you care about? In what ways do you pretend you're all right when you're not? Have you ever shared your situation with someone and immediately regretted doing so? What did sharing it cost you? What does hiding it cost you?

◆ In what areas of your life do you have choices that you're not exercising? What are you tolerating, big or small, that is within your power to change? What's the story you tell yourself that prevents you from taking action? How does doing nothing serve you?

◆ Is your network truly your real net worth? Is being part of a community essential to your happiness? Are your friendships and community more important to you now than in the past? Do you invest in family members and friends, make time for them, check in regularly, etc.? Is it really true that you don't have time to nurture the relationships that matter to you? When was the last time you made a new friend? Who initiated the relationship?

◆ A survey by the nonprofit Transamerica Center for Retirement Studies found that only "41 percent of boomers say they've kept their job skills up to date."[24] Are you among those who have or who have not? Are you a curious person open to learning new things? What new skills have you learned/taken up in the last year? If you can't remember the last time you've learned anything new, check this out: http://www.lifehack.org/383948/15-websites-learn-skill-your-own-time-without-disturbing-your-schedule. There's also One Day University, live talks around the country given by top professors. These lectures are geared toward people over fifty and are a fun way to learn. At $95 to $159, these live talks can be pricey, but all lectures are available online for $12. https://www.onedayu.com.

♦ What are you prepared to consider in your third act that would have been out of the question five years ago? For example, housing: Could you relocate to another city? Could you take in a house or apartment mate? What if you had to share a bathroom? Could you sell the house you've lived in for twenty-seven years? Could you live in a one-room studio apartment? You don't necessarily want to do any of these things, but what would it take for you to be genuinely OK with and open to living differently—perhaps radically so—from how you live now?

Chapter 5

Grabbing Denial by the Lapels

I have been fortunate. I have been poor for quite a long time now, so I'm pretty good at it. The simple no-frills life is fine by me.

—Debie

Millions of us are trying to wrap our brains around futures that look nothing like the ones we imagined. How do we walk up that hill? It's about letting go of what used to be and figuring out what we need to do and to change now so that we can have a shot at a more satisfying life in our fourth quarter.

You may not like all of the things that I invite you to consider and take on in the chapters ahead. Adaptation is hard at any age, but it's especially hard now, as all of the rules are changing just as we boomers are planning our endgames. It would be so much easier just to do what we've always done.

But we can't. We're anxious and uncertain about the future, and just scraping by for the next thirty years is not going to cut it. Nor is being mired in some old stuck story or feeling mad, bitter, and crotchety. All of those "wouldas, couldas, and shouldas" are just a waste of precious time at this point.

The bottom line is that we are where we are. And it's from here that we start. While there is no one-size-fits-all solution to the challenges we're facing, there is much we can learn from our peers who are experimenting with unconventional approaches and innovative ways of relating to others, consuming goods, and working to find security and happiness.

If we're in denial, resistant to change, or unwilling to consider anything new or outside of our comfort zones, we might as well close up shop now. How we start this exploration matters. Staying open and hanging loose are important.

I have to say one thing. You cannot have a victim mentality or you might as well not get up in the morning. The days of cushy desk jobs, ordering lunch every day, and fat paychecks might be over, but you have to keep pushing. If you have "friends" who go to bars and restaurants that you can't afford, find some new friends who enjoy a cup of coffee and a chat instead. Learn how to be self-sufficient and enjoy the things in life that cost less. Stop reading the don't-want-you ads, and try to do something else.

—Tracy

The Cavalry Ain't Coming

Where we start is by recognizing that the cavalry is not coming to rescue us. There is no national bailout, no Prince Charming on a white horse.

In the short to medium term, we're going to have to save ourselves and one another.

Why? Well, with few exceptions, our politicians are not offering comprehensive solutions to the retirement income crisis. Most are focused on social security as though it were *the* answer and *the* magic bullet. But what if you're one of the millions of boomers under the full-retirement age of between sixty-five or sixty-seven, depending on when you were born? Then, for now, you're out. Receiving the full social security benefit isn't even an option.

And even when you are eligible for it, the full benefit will replace only about 40 percent of your preretirement income—if that. Most financial advisors say you'll need 70 to 80 percent of it to maintain your standard of living. For tens of millions of Americans, that small social security check is the only money coming in. Our lawmakers can pretend all they want that that's enough to live on. Give me a break.

And while we welcome the recent talk in Washington about increasing the social security benefit, we also know that the wheels of change turn slowly. Meanwhile, we're living in the meantime.

And exhorting us to simply save more without telling us how to do it doesn't help us, either.

I went with my sister to one of those financial planning seminars and had to leave the room a few times because I was so upset by what I was hearing. It was just so sobering. I have no savings. The planner kept talking about putting 30 percent of your assets into this or that thing. Well, 30 percent of zero is zero.

—Chris

It will take years for our government and institutions to find and scale solutions to the myriad of problems that underlie the retirement income crisis. And as those most affected by the crisis, part of our job is pressuring them to do more and to do it faster.

But in the meantime, with no big interventions in the works, our immediate focus should be on what we can do for ourselves.

Saying Good-bye to Magical Thinking

So, where do we start? We start by dismantling the belief that if we just tough it out, things will return to normal. The truth is that we're not going back. The normal we knew is gone.

In "normal land," we could zig and zag, move, change jobs or spouses, try new things, and still recover from our mistakes. We had time. Now, in our late fifties, sixties, and beyond, we don't have that time anymore.

"Normal" was when we had money and did not have to weigh our every decision against its affordability.

Normal was before we knew anyone trapped in their homes, unable to move because their mortgage was underwater.

It was before we were outsourced, merged, downsized, rifted, and surplused.

In normal land, the "sharing economy" had mostly not been invented yet. Instead, there were good W-2 jobs with pensions and benefits.

In normal land, we measured our worth by our incomes, props, and credentials. For some of us, working hard assured a nice retirement "dessert" of travel and kicked-back living.

Normal was when we weren't worried about our children's futures. As one friend put it, we figured we'd done our jobs if our adult children were employed and could afford their own therapy.

Normal land had material perks too. There was stuff and more stuff. Back in those days, designer labels mattered more than the factory workers who made those labels.

Before marketers coined the term HENRY, or "high earners not rich yet," there were yuppies and buppies. A good life of achievement and acquisition was what most of us aspired to and sought.

Magical thinking is believing that the old normal is coming back.

The New Normal of Financial Vulnerability

Right now, depending on your work situation or bank account, you may feel like a tourist in the land of the poor people. At this stage, your main goal is to avoid getting trapped and having to take up permanent residency there. It is a paralyzing thought. I know.

This happened to me in my forties, and it took me a good ten years to get back to a normal wage. It took periods of working three jobs at crummy wages and doing whatever I had to do to keep going. The truth is your friends don't notice the struggle, because they fear it will happen to them. Decide who your genuine friends are and come clean to them. If nothing else, it will help to talk about it and frees you up from pretending. This is more widespread than most people think.

—Linda

You see friends who used to be doing nicely off-ramped with no clear path back to normal. You see it in their faces. It's like they have dematerialized.

Most of the women (and men) I worked with who suffered a similar fate never seemed to quite get back to where they were, even though they worked as hard as I did and even in the booming tech market. And I pretty much expect every day that this could happen to me again, no matter how hard I work or how many points I put on the board. The worst part is the isolation. This is the first time I have ever let on how bad it was (is), and it still feels extremely risky to do so in a valley rife with swagger.

—J

And you know that if it happened to others, it could happen to you. No longer in denial now, you actually begin to contemplate what would happen if the bottom totally fell out. What would you do? How would you survive?

And millions of us aren't contemplating it; we're living it.

I am at the fifteen-year mark of my uphill climb out of my hole. I am living tiny, but it is mine, and I am able to live within my means.

—Richard

Many of us won't be making the money we're used to making. For the first time we will be facing the prospect of significant downward mobility, with our accustomed earnings cut by 20, 30, 40 percent—or more.

I never had to resort to food stamps but was headed that way and am still rattled to the core by that.

—Linda

When you are unemployed long term and the money runs out, you find that there is nowhere you can be. Every place of refuge and rest costs money. An apartment, a car—even a seat at Starbucks—costs something. You begin to feel like you have no place in the world, and that has been the hardest thing for me.

—James

If we lose our jobs in our fifties and sixties, we're unlikely to be reemployed at the same salaries we had before. This is true even for those whose career choice privilege has, until now, firmly established them in the high five- or six-figure salary range.

Sure, a few of us will manage to find traditional W-2 jobs paying that long bread like before. But many more of us can expect months or even years of unemployment that deplete our savings and shake our confidence.

And when we do work again, we'll likely do contract work in the gig economy or some part-time jobs in new professions.

I am single, sixty-four, getting social security, and working whatever jobs I can find that pay the bills. I'm finally in a job I like now, but it has taken years to get to this place. During those years, I worked in factories, in retail, and at a gas station, and I did home care. You name it and I've done it. I'm tired of job hopping to survive.

—Anita

I drive a school bus, have a class B CDL with a passenger/ school bus endorsement, and feel lucky to have a job. I was a music-ed teacher. You gotta lose your pride and get out there and start somewhere. I am sixty-one and was married to a doc-

*tor for twenty-three years, and I got divorced ten years ago. Pull
up your big-girl pants and take whatever job(s) you can find.*

—Brenda

Some people start entrepreneurial ventures to try to make ends
meet. Whatever we do, we're looking at a lot less money to live on,
at least in the short term—and maybe forever.

That's why a big first step in securing our futures is adopting a
live-low-to-the-ground mind-set, which means that we have to drastically cut our expenses to fit our new income realities.

I know, I know: that sounds easy peasy. You're thinking, *How
hard could it really be to live within your new means?*

It's true that reality forces most people to make the needed changes
eventually. But that click down from the standard of living that you
assumed you'd always have to one that is much more modest is . . .
well, it's an adjustment. And it's a big adjustment if you were living
large and are now scrambling just to cover the basic necessities.

But a downgrade in lifestyle is hard not only for the people who
were doing well; it's hard for everybody. Most folks just don't have
that much of a cushion. The Pew Charitable Trusts' 2015 Survey of
American Family Finances found that "the median household does
not have enough in liquid savings—money held in checking and savings accounts, unused balances on prepaid cards, and cash saved at
home—to replace one month of income." [1]

And the average family in the lowest income quintile is even
worse off, with less than two weeks of financial reserves—or, to be
exact, enough to cover about nine days' worth of expenses. [2]

And nothing's changed. Updates to this data reported by Pew in
2017 don't present a different picture. The typical American family
still can't "replace even one month of income with liquid savings . . ." [3]

So, as we look into the future, the key question will not be how to
tighten our belts or live within our means in the conventional sense.
In the new normal of financial insecurity, a lot of us are already doing
that.

The real question is: Can we cut way back and still have good quality of life, still find ways to be connected to who and what we love?

I believe that the short answer is yes. But to have a shot at something other than being old and poor in America, we can't just do what we've always done and be what we've always been. The world as we knew it has changed forever. And if we want better futures, we're going to have to change too.

Meet Zoe

When I met with Zoe, who was sixty-two at the time, she had $31 to her name—*literally*. And I had never seen her happier or more grounded and anchored. Yes, she had landed a new client, and money was in the pipeline, but in June she was still on food stamps and living in a one-bedroom rental in a Maryland suburb.

Her career, which had included international business travel, high-profile clients, a testimony before Congress, and a group Emmy, began to unravel during the great recession of 2007–2009. "I am as broke now as I was back then," she said. "I didn't climb out of a hole and go back to my old life, but I have found an inner peace that was out of reach before."

That old life included a 2,500-square-foot four-level home on a tree-lined street in a tony Washington, DC, suburb; enough china to host a party for forty; and several investment-quality Persian silk carpets, one of which was large enough to cover her fourteen-by-eighteen-foot living room.

The great recession happened on the heels of her divorce, delivering a one-two punch. At fifty-eight, she found that her work opportunities had all but dried up. Without clients, things spiraled out of control. "I was under so much pressure. I couldn't sleep. I'd hear a noise at night and jump up and run to the window, expecting to see the repo man pulling out of the driveway with my car."

Today she admits that, back then, she spent all of her energy on getting her old life back, her old identity. "My focus was all on the external," she said. "My idea of success was a personal relationship with the sales staff at Bloomingdale's, concierge services, and being greeted by name when I walked into a congressional office."

After the economy tanked, money came together in dribs and drabs. She'd land a couple of small contracts and then nothing for months. "I was always digging out of a hole. When a check did finally come, I'd need it, and more, to pay back bills."

Meanwhile, she was still trying to play the part. That meant saying yes when colleagues got together for nightcaps after working late or picking up the dinner tab with a potential client. "Of course, no one ever suggested T.G.I. Friday's, Ruby Tuesdays, or Olive Garden," she said, laughing. It was always the chicest DC watering holes, where one drink and a couple of "small" plates would easily run you $50 and up with tax and tip.

"In those days I was afraid to say no," Zoe said. "I was tap-dancing as fast as I could, but the income just never came together again consistently enough for me to reproduce my old life."

By the spring of 2013, she was three months behind on her house payments. She packed up her stuff and rented a storage unit large enough to hold the contents of her four-bedroom house and moved in with family members in another city.

She was grateful to have somewhere to go, but the change was stark. "My college-aged daughter and I went from living in about two thousand five hundred square feet of space to seven hundred square feet of space."

Those were dark days. All she wanted to do was hide. In her eyes, the move broadcast failure. "I was in shock, embarrassed, and lost. I cried all the time. My identity had been defined by the high-profile jobs and all my stuff.

"God needed to strip me down to the essentials," she said. "I was valuing all the wrong things. I would have never moved out of that big house voluntarily even when it was clear I couldn't afford it. My identity was too tied up in being there."

Living with her family, she was separated from everything that had mattered to her: her work, her house, her lifestyle, and her identity.

"What I realized was that I'd never owned all of the things that I'd thought were mine in the first place. Bank of America owned my house, Capital One owned my car, and my clients were owned by the corporations that employed them."

Up until the move, she'd felt in control. No matter how chaotic things had become, she'd always been able to figure out the next step. "Now the way forward was no longer clear, and it spooked me. Strategies that used to be failproof I couldn't depend on anymore."

Nothing worked.

"I was grieving the loss of things that had never really belonged to me. I needed a break from all the scrambling and running in place. I was pushing so hard that I couldn't think. I realized that the only thing I 'owned' was myself, but not in the ways I'd thought. I realized I had control over only two things: my plan for what I wanted to happen and how I'd respond to what had actually happened. Ultimately, what actually happened was out of my control. What actually happened was in God's hands."

Zoe said that that was something she'd always realized intellectually, but she had never been tested the way she was being tested now. She'd been humbled by the situation. And out of this humility had come a kind of quiet that allowed her to access a part of herself that was not driven by status and money.

"I recommitted to those things I could control: daily meditation and yoga, exercise and diet. I'd been meditating off and on for twenty-five years, but in the chaos of my situation I returned to a daily practice. When you're broke, you're in a perpetual state of fear and panic. You're always anticipating the worst. But an hour of yoga gives you a place of rest, and the rhythmic breathing clears everything. Your head and heart are clear enough to hear the still, quiet voice of God."

Laughing, Zoe continued. "There were days when I wanted to jump from my family's front porch, but it was only five feet off the ground." The breathing strategy she learned in meditation helped her walk back from the ledge.

Zoe sought out ways to improve herself and to grow her business. She worked out daily at the YMCA—which offered her a sliding-scale rate based on her income—did yoga classes on YouTube, and visited one of the neighborhood yoga studios twice a month.

One of her biggest finds was the Maryland Small Business Association, which offers people assistance on everything from creating business plans to registering businesses, establishing banking relationships, and creating effective websites. "Working with my business counselor gave me hope that I would work again.

"Help is available, but you have to look for it, and you have to ask," Zoe said. "I found that virtually all creditors will work with you if you tell them what's going on. But you have to ask and ask more than once about programs for people facing hardships, because lots of times this information is not volunteered.

"I also signed up for food stamps. A lot of people who need food stamps and qualify for them are too ashamed to get them. Don't be ridiculous," she said. "Government programs are there as a hand up."

At her family's house, Zoe mined her assets. On a big whiteboard, she listed all the things she excelled at and everything she loved doing.

Nowadays she's focused more on what she wants to do than on what others think she should be doing. "I am building a casserole of work more aligned with my values. Of course, I still get the occasional crap client whom I have to take for the money, but I am trying to create a life where that's the exception, not the rule."

Despite her more steady income, Zoe's goal is not to return to the high monthly overhead she faced before. "I am always looking for more ways to cut expenses. The day I stopped getting calls from creditors was my first day of freedom in years."

While writing a check for her storage unit, she realized that after a year she could not recall what was in the unit. "I couldn't think of a single thing I was missing. Not once had I wondered where such-and-such was. I realized everything I needed to make my life work was already with me."

No longer missing her possessions, she called her family and friends and sold or gave away everything that did not have a deep meaning for her. Within three weeks she created another level of emotional and economic freedom: the freedom to leave a client she hated.

A month later she called Capital One and conducted a voluntary repossession of her automobile. Laughing, she says, "I'll never forget the look on their faces when I pulled into that lot to give them their car back." The car note, insurance payments, and gasoline were costing $1,000 a month. Now that she was able to catch up on her car payments, she no longer wanted the expense.

Zipcar, Uber, and the subway now take care of her transportation needs. "Yeah, I took a hit to my credit rating, but it was worth it. I got my freedom back."

Her one-bedroom apartment is airy and bright and decorated

with her favorite pieces from her old life. She recently landed a short-term contract that allows her to pay the bills with a little money to spare. Life is good in a deeply satisfying way—but not because she has her old life back.

"What I know is that life can flip on you in an instant. I take nothing for granted. My money is still lumpy and inconsistent. But I am out of debt. I have an apartment, not a house, and I don't own a car. I have no savings, and the future is fuzzy. But I met *me* in this process. The real me. Yes, the price has been steep but worth it."

Here Is What I Learned From Zoe:

Live Low to the Ground

You inventory your closet and discover that you really don't need twelve pairs of black pants and seventeen pairs of shoes.

You look at your home and find that there's a lot that you love and a bunch of stuff that you could do without.

Depending on the financial pressure you're under, everything might be on the chopping block—including the $400 monthly fee that you're paying for storage, the second car, and that $750 mobile phone. You start thinking about dropping Verizon and going with one of those fixed-fee no-name providers.

You do whatever you have to do to get your expenses down, down, and down some more.

Think Strategy, Not Failure

If you need food stamps, get the darn food stamps. If you need to get rid of that gas-guzzling SUV, do it. If you need to move in with your sister temporarily to avert the avalanche, pick up the phone and call her.

Think of these things as just strategic choices. It's what you have to do to secure yourself. It's what you have to do to go another round.

You're not going to like it. You're not going to want to do it. You're going to privately fall to pieces more than once. You're going to take to your bed.

But you're going to get through it by putting one foot in front of the other.

A Daily Centering Practice

Zoe's centering practice involved yoga and meditation. You might lean on daily prayer and your faith in God. For someone else, that practice might be a morning run or meeting three friends at McDonald's for a cup of coffee every Tuesday.

It is hitting the pause button. It is finding a place to reflect on your life, to go inward, to go deep, and to be quiet. It is remembering who you were before all the chaos.

It is making time for that friend who reminds you of what you're worth. It is listening to his or her stories, witnessing him or her, and being validated.

Taking Advantage of the Downtime

Zoe used her months off the grid to take care of some practical business matters. For example, while working with the Maryland Small Business Association, she applied to have her business certified as a woman-owned business. When things began to turn around, that designation opened up opportunities for her.

What on your list can you get done during your down period? What box can you check off?

Zoe also used this time to restructure her company and to focus on the work and the clients that gave her the most joy.

Resilience Circle Reflection

Dispensing with Magical Thinking

Remember to do the "Top This" exercise and to have three minutes of silence.

Making fundamental changes is hard, yet that's what we have to do. It's much easier to risk nothing and to forfeit what control we do have over our lives. But that's not the only scenario. What other paths might we walk?

- What is your "stuck" story? Most of us have one. What's yours? Is it only a lack of money that's holding you back? Can you envision a better life for yourself? Is that something that you still see as possible?

- What does a good life entail for you? Skip the trite answers and go deeper. Don't say "family" if you haven't spoken to your siblings in two years and don't miss them. Don't say "X" if you never actually do X. What really matters to you may be very different from what matters to the person sitting across from you. Name two or three things that matter to you and then ask yourself whether those things, experiences, or relationships are really out of reach. Or are there trade-offs you'd rather not make? For example, I could afford one small trip a year if I rented out my second bedroom, but I don't really want to rent it out.

- What's the difference between magical thinking and a positive attitude? And how do you know when you're engaging in one and not the other? A fifty-eight-year-old friend who's been looking for a job for eighteen months turned one down recently because it paid 40 percent less than what he's used to making, and he didn't want to mess up his salary history. Is that optimism about future job prospects or magical thinking?

- What magical thinking are you still holding on to even when nothing in your life supports your belief that X, Y, or Z is ever coming back? Are you still holding on to an income you used to make, an activity you used to routinely engage in, or a place you used to go? What's this magical thinking costing you? Are you missing any opportunities because you're focused on getting back what's not coming back?

Chapter 6

Smalling Up: Rethinking Limits, Lack, and Deprivation

I lost my job and benefits at forty-eight. Then I lost my health. I maxed out my $5,000 deductible, not to mention my premiums. Guess what? I lost a lot of friends, too—the kind who complained about who their tennis partners were going to be at the club. The kind who worried about what $75,000 colleges their children would be attending. The kind whose biggest decisions were where the family vacations would be. The kind who looked forward to spending the summer at their beach houses. But I also made new friends. The kind who care. The kind who saw me through the surgeries. The kind who invite me to their houses for nice dinners. I've learned what kindness really is. I've learned to be there for people I never thought I had anything in common with. I've learned to go with the flow. I still have problems, but I have friends who care. I'm counting my blessings.

—Barbara

When we hear *cut back* or *downsize*, we cringe. Many of us think lower standards of living, failure, limits, lack, and deprivation. The only way we're going there is kicking and screaming, with our nails clawing the floor.

You've told me that you don't want to move from the place you've lived in for years. You don't want to put cherished items in storage or couch surf at your brother's pad or take big chunks out of the little money you've managed to save to survive.

You say that you hate how far from the city you might have to move to make ends meet. You absolutely refuse to get a roommate. You panicked when your unemployment benefits ran out. No way are you applying for food stamps. You dodge friends who've loaned you money, because you're still too broke to pay them back.

You use words like *loser* and *failure* to describe what you have become. One of you said that you felt like you were "swirling around the abyss."

What if instead of digging in, resisting change, and fighting every step, we looked at these changes through the lens of strategy and opportunity?

When Zoe faced a major work gap and unstable income at the age of sixty-two, she ditched her car in favor of public transportation, saving nearly $1,000 per month in car-note payments, gas, maintenance costs, and registration and insurance costs.

A year before, she would have been ashamed to return the car to the dealer. Back then, she would have "faked normal" and made up some fictional story about why she needed to get rid of her car.

Today she's pocketing the extra $1,000 per month and is doing fine. That's strategy, not deprivation.

Kate, a successful fifty-eight-year-old marketing executive who has seen better times, moved from her stunning 3,000-square-foot-home in Atlanta to a small six-hundred-square-foot rental in a Maryland suburb. I asked her how she'd made the change work.

"There's no magic to it," she said. "What choice did I have? I did what I had to do."

And what she did was turn a small, modest apartment into a home. Her art is up on the walls, and textiles and decorative pillows are scattered about. Obviously she couldn't bring all of her furniture, but the core of her personality is still reflected in her home. She brought the pieces she loved and mixed them in with inexpensive accessories from Ikea and Target.

She "smalled up." She figured out what mattered to her and what she could afford and got rid of the rest.

I smalled up last year when I decided to attend a dear friend's destination black-tie wedding in Savannah, Georgia. I couldn't afford to fly, so I hitched a ride with some friends making the ten-hour trek by car. I didn't stay in the designated hotel, which was way outside my budget. I bunked with a roommate in a moderate hotel a few miles away.

In my old life, I spent a small fortune on clothes, but I didn't buy a dress for this wedding. I shopped in my closet instead, having learned to utilize my own surplus.

I'm not telling you that all of this isn't an adjustment. And depending on how large you were living before your personal financial crisis hit, the adjustment could be big.

My "modest" hotel—nicer than a Motel 6 but below a Holiday Inn—was not located in the historic district of Savannah, with its artists' lofts, quaint cafés, and highbrow food markets. Where I stayed was surrounded by car dealerships and strip malls. There was no leisurely brunch with old friends who were attending the wedding. Breakfast for me meant orange juice from a concentrate and dry scrambled eggs kept warm under a heat lamp and served on a paper plate.

But here is what it also meant. The *total* cost of my three-day weekend, including travel, food, and lodging, was less than $200, instead of the $1,200-plus it would have cost me had I flown down, stayed in the designated wedding hotel, and hung out the way I had in my "old" life.

And I had a wonderful time. I met with old friends in the historic district over four-dollar cups of coffee instead of fifty-five-dollar brunches and catching up with them was just as good—just as magical—as it had been before. The point is that I got to be there for a dear friend of twenty-five years and to witness her have the wedding she'd always wanted.

Showing up matters. I want to be there for the big things in life and for a lot of the small things too. And isn't that where many of us boomers are now: figuring out what trade-offs we have to make for that to happen? I was not going to miss my friend's wedding because I couldn't fly to the destination or afford to buy a new dress.

~~Mourning~~ Managing Our Losses

Is it hard? Yes, especially in the beginning. You're going to experience profound feelings of loss, dislocation, upset, and sadness if you're among those used to plopping down your company credit card to pay for four- and five-star hotels and turning left instead of right when you board an international flight. You are going to feel the changes, and they're going to rock you.

Regardless of how you were living before you landed here, you're not going to be thrilled about seeing your standard of living drop. But that's the reality that tens of millions of boomers are facing.

So we have a choice to make. We can focus all of our attention on the doors that have closed behind us, or we can turn around and explore what's possible in front of us.

Because, really, what's the point of all of that bitching, moaning, and kvetching about what used to be? What do we gain exactly from clutching our pearls and complaining ad nauseam about where we've landed? It gets us nothing. It changes nothing. And when it's all said and done, we don't even feel better afterward.

Since millions of us can no longer afford the lives we led with all of that stuff, isn't it preferable to decide what we're ready to let go of than have that choice made for us? Isn't it better to build upon our decades of accumulated knowledge to forge our new futures? Isn't having agency in our own lives and being proactive, even if we are taking tiny steps at first, better than sitting back and being victims?

Figuring Out What Matters

Meaning is not something you stumble across, like an answer to a riddle or the prize in a treasure hunt. Meaning is something you build into your life. You build it out of your own past, out of your affections and loyalties, out of the experience of humankind as it is passed on to you, out of your own talent and understanding, out of the things you believe in and the people you love, out of values for which you are willing to sacrifice something. The ingredients are there. You are the only one who can put them together in that unique pattern that will be your life. Let it be a life that has meaning and dignity for you. If it does, then the particular balance of success or failure is of less account.

—John W. Gardner, former Secretary of Health,
Education, and Welfare

The economics of aging is already pushing millions of us to reevaluate what is important to us and what gives our lives meaning. With shrinking incomes, we're forced to take hard looks at how we're living and what we're spending our money on.

By now we get that life is more than a checklist of acquisitions. But in the new normal of financial insecurity, we are called to know in a deeper way what it really means to live a life not defined by things.

Here's what you've told me: after some months of functioning with a lot less disposable income, you notice that you don't miss some things as much as you thought you would. These are small things at first, like cable television, movies, quick stops at your favorite fast-food joint, designer coffees, and $36 entrées at your favorite Michelin-rated restaurant.

No longer able to drop $5, $50, or $500 on impulse purchases, you become more conscious and more intentional about what you're buying. Do you really want that $5 slice of pizza, that magazine, or that $28 T-shirt? Do you really want to pay $15 for valet parking?

In the old normal, some of us used money to buy the emotions that we desired to feel. Looking to escape boredom, emptiness, and the mundane, we shopped for all kinds of "non-necessities."

Those souped-up gadgets tell the world that we're still fierce and fab. Being greeted by name at that new neighborhood eatery says that we belong. That new purse, jacket, pair of shoes, or slacks (you fill in the blank) bestows on us the confidence that we wish we naturally had. Going for the custom interior on a new Chevrolet Silverado supports the sense that we're special.

This is a lot of us. Luckily, I downsized homes and cars and have a meager pension, $200, but it's something, and it's more than most have, and it pays for food. I am really thinking about tiny homes/RV lifestyles. I think people (most are young) have learned something watching us struggle. At the end of the day, a purse doesn't bring you happiness; neither does having a bunch of stuff.

—Faith

When we're broke, we can't chase these illusions. There is no place for want-driven spending on nonessential things. Stripped down to the basics, we finally have to face ourselves and who we are without our props and credentials. As J. K. Rowling said, "Rock bottom became the solid foundation on which I rebuilt my life."

The decision to live low to the ground also gives us the opportunity to pause before making rote choices, to figure out what matters to us now, and to think about how we want to spend our limited resources.

You will surprise yourself. Some of your habitual responses about who you are and what you need to be happy will ring hollow. You will find that what was true for you at forty-two is not necessarily true at sixty-two.

After having it all, doing it all, and being it all, there comes a time in everyone's life where they finally reach the age of sanity, which is the realization that none of it ever really mattered. When the kids move out, you retire, sell your home, and move away, and you see just how full of crap your life was. You settle into an 830-square-foot condo from a huge house; go Zen; remove everything that took up space and filled closets and drawers; and get rid of the garage full of holiday decorations, the nuts and bolts and multiple screwdrivers, the kitchen stacked with the latest gadgets, and the bookshelves filled with dusty reads waiting to catch fire. There is freedom in letting it all go. Let it go. We're not what we have or the letters after our last names. What defines you as a person is not your stuff, titles, ownership, or collections. The choices we have and are given to make, the freedom to choose, and the ability to overcome and rise up from our choices is freedom. Living "under" our means, sharing our knowledge and wisdom with others, making a difference in others' lives, living simply, and sowing the seeds in empty fields are extraordinary gifts.

—Anita

Living What Matters

The "decision" to live a more materially frugal, inner-directed life is not made overnight.

Finding happiness and joy in nontraditional ways of living, consuming goods, and working is a process. And the details of your journey are likely to be different from mine.

Even now I find myself shuttling back and forth between old habits and the conscious simplicity that I am seeking now.

My earthy-crunchier friends beat me up for still shopping at big-box retailers and swear that some child is slaving away somewhere, chained to a sewing machine, so that I can get those rock-bottom prices.

I have always liked clothes as storytelling devices. I learned early on that the right outfit could buy me an additional five- to seven-minute grace period in which to make an impression—and that was a valuable lesson for a young black girl growing up in the sixties and seventies.

> *Even as a black girl, I knew my brain could take me places. If I couldn't catch Tom, Dick, or Harry, I knew I could at least catch their shirt.*
>
> —Joyce

But these days I'm not doing a lot of shopping for new clothes. I wear what I already own or buy hand-me-downs in better consignment shops, amazed at what people are discarding.

And I have discovered fast fashion at Zara, H&M, and Forever 21, which should really be called Forever 55. Why spend $28 to replace a white cotton T-shirt when you can spend $5.

I'm learning that living low to the ground doesn't need to be drab, barren, or dull. I don't have to live isolated in a mud hut in the rural countryside.

I don't have to reject technology.

I do use things longer.

I can still embrace art and culture. I get to keep my most cherished paintings, tapestries, and crafts that I collected over forty years of travel.

I didn't have to downsize my residence. I still live in the small house I've lived in for the last thirty or so years. The neighborhood, though, is much improved. In fact, I couldn't afford to buy here if I were looking for housing today.

I drive one of those "scary" little vehicles that my grandson describes as more of a sled than a car. It's a Fiat 500, the kind of car you saw Pope Francis tooling around in during his 2015 US tour.

My good diet has become even better, with more home-prepared meals and fresh ingredients.

I used to eat out a lot, but as I'm on a much tighter budget now, I've had to cut back drastically, and that's something that I still miss.

Each of us has those things that we do or buy without which we would feel deprived. For me, those things are dinners out and wearable art. For you, they will be something else, like your YETI cooler, or collection of Milwaukee power tools, or theater tickets—whatever material things or experiences make your heart sing.

Gardening is my church on Sunday. I'm not even that great at it. I just so enjoy the peace. Nothing centers me more.

—Madison

Years ago, I had a friend who'd buy barely running secondhand cars to tool around in, but he would scrimp and save to spend $17,000 on a flute, because playing music with that wood instrument was his true love.

Many of my friends have high-end stoves. The last time I boiled an egg, the water evaporated and the egg exploded in the pan. A gourmet cook I am not. When I redid my kitchen ten years ago, a fancy-schmancy oven was not a priority.

Living low to the ground means figuring out what matters to you and what your priorities are and then cutting *way* back on everything else.

I'm fifty-nine years old and have the same story as the others. Now I'm serving twenty-seven months in Peru with the Peace Corps. I have a stipend and free medical care. Plus it's engaging and fun.

—Jan

Confusing Wants with Needs

We live in a culture that creates need where none existed before and defines quality of life as a metric of income. When you're making money, all of that mindless consumption goes unnoticed and unchecked. When funds are tight, you have to think about it. What do you really need to feel deeply grounded and content? You'll discover that you actually need very little. It really does not cost much to be happy.

> *All I need [to be content] is to sit under a tree, drink a beer, and eat jerk chicken with flip-flops, a T-shirt, a pair of shorts, and a little cap on.*
>
> —Edward

> *I live comfortably on about $30,000 a year in one of the most expensive places in the country and don't really want for anything. Yeah, I could use a replacement TV for the one that blew out in a big thunderstorm, but, yeah, I can skip watching TV in the kitchen awhile until I save enough money to buy a new one. No big deal, unless you live by the philosophy that you gotta have everything you want the instant you want it.*
>
> —Brad

Good health, family, and friends do it for me. And giving up "life in a hurry" has helped as well. Meaningful work matters, too, but we'll get to that later.

I'm not going to tell you that working out to a YouTube exercise video is as good as working out in a well-equipped gym. But under financial pressure, your body pays the price. Stress takes a heavy toll on people, showing up as depleted energy, sallow skin, thinning hair, and weight gain or loss.

Nothing broadcasts your sudden reversal of fortune more than looking "tore up from the floor up," let alone what it can do to your self-esteem.

> *I got rid of the nail salon habit and let my hair grow long, qualified for and used food stamps, and semiretired to a warmer climate.*
>
> —Jeannie

So no expensive gym membership for me, but I have kept myself together by bouncing around my living room for free with YouTube exercise gurus like Tiffany Rothe, which has saved me thousands in gym membership dues.

I have also gone to free gyms managed by the DC government. Check out your local department of parks and recreation. True, the equipment in those gyms is sometimes a little older, but free is free.

I'm spending a tiny fraction of what I used to spend on entertainment, and the world hasn't ended. Spending more time with my grandson costs nothing. He doesn't love me less because I'm not buying him the latest sneakers or electronics. Connecting with my daughter over a home-cooked spaghetti supper is free.

Friends meet for happy hours, when drinks are half-price. It's also not uncommon for two of us to split the cost of an entrée or to enjoy only hors d'oeuvres to save dollars.

But, mostly, friends are bypassing restaurants altogether in favor of dinners at home, with everyone pitching in. We're as connected as ever: laughing and carrying on, sprawled out on the floor, comfortable in our stocking feet, drinking $7 bottles of wine we cost shared from Trader Joe's.

The women friends I rely on for sanity are all still here. It turns out that we didn't need fine dining and $12 glasses of Chardonnay to bond us.

By working all of the pulleys and levers, you'll figure out what makes sense for you. But first you have to know *what you need at a bare minimum* to be happy, and then you need to investigate alternative ways to keep those things in your life. It's never going to look like it did before, but even in the midst of ongoing money drama, you can create a rich and textured life.

Home is where my Wi-Fi launches automatically. I used to care what zip code I lived in, but eight years ago my husband and I got rid of all our stuff and sold our home in Atlanta and our apartment in New York. Got rid of the Prius too. We're never buying a house again. I've had to redefine luxury. A home is no longer a refuge for me. A big house is a trap. One safety deposit box and a small storage unit contain all of my most important possessions.

—Skylar

How to Stop Buying Crap That You Don't Need

I like Larry Winget's book *You're Broke Because You Want to Be: How to Stop Getting By and Start Getting Ahead.* Larry does not just step on your toes—he stomps on both of your feet, drags you through the coals, and calls you names.

His book is full of blunt talk for those of us who are faking normal, fronting big time, and clinging to lifestyles we can no longer afford.

Keep in mind that the book was published in 2008, so some parts may sound . . . well, *quaint* in light of current technological advances. Winget also tends to blame the victim: the shock-and-awe approach is his style. I ignored that part, and you should too.

But if you are someone who's having trouble ducking and rolling off the treadmill of excessive spending, Larry Winget's book may be the kick in the pants that you need.

The "Smugtocracy" of Modest Living

I have found that there is a kind of "smugtocracy" around living a modest lifestyle. Those who manage to live on $10,000 or even less per year (yes, apparently that's doable, based on books I've seen) are critical and sometimes even scornful of people who have figured out how to live on $20,000 per annum. The $20,000 folks positively mock and roll their eyes at those who say that they need $40,000 per annum to live reasonably comfortable lifestyles, and so on.

Ignore all of them. Don't get shamed into getting rid of the things that you cherish.[1] You decide what makes sense for you based on your wallet, current circumstances, priorities, and soul. I am not someone who will build my own house, make my own clothes, and grow my own food to save money. I experience that as extreme renunciation, and it won't work for me.

But it may be right for you. Only you can decide what's best for you.

I was in Barbados recently, staying in a very modest guesthouse on the beach. The room was not much bigger than the dining room table in my old house. I slept with the door open, awaking each morning to the sound of the waves lapping the shore. I have surrendered the idea that my path is written. No sharp turns is my goal at this stage of my life, and to live as graciously as possible. I am optimistic about the future. My brother could always take me in if it came to that. I also have a bunch of friends with spare rooms, but I don't think I'll need them.

—Skylar

I Am No Eco-Warrior

A few years back I attended a workshop in Vermont at the Center for Whole Communities (CWC) at Knoll Farm. CWC is known for its focus on living in harmony with the natural environment. I somehow missed the memo that said our lodging for the weekend would be in tents on the farm's grounds. So this city girl who barely walks in the grass arrived in high heels and full makeup. Fellow participants swung into gear and lent me tennis shoes, galoshes, shorts, and T-shirts.

All around the accommodations were small, unexpected touches of luxury: a bar of lavender soap, a scented candle, inspirational words on signposts, fresh-cut flowers, a handcrafted wood bowl, and fresh-picked blueberries from the farm. I remember being afraid to open the compost toilet, sure that I'd faint from the stench, but there was no smell at all.

Now, I'm no eco-warrior and won't be moving to a farm. But CWC gave me a glimpse at another way of being in the world that balances personal satisfaction with sustainable living. Over the course of my career, I have stayed in four- and five-star hotels all over the globe. None gave me the sense of satisfaction and contentment that I felt when I left Knoll Farm.

I didn't expect any aspects of a more modest lifestyle to appeal to me, but many of them did. I believe millions of us will have no choice but to "small up" and get on board.

Meet Abe

This is Abe's story in his own words:

After all these years, I still lose sleep thinking about how much of my up-and-down work experience—the slow burnout of my thirty-five-plus'-year career as a marketing professional—is my fault, attributable to some personality quirk or motivational shortcoming, and how much is due to external factors beyond my control.

At sixty-two, I have not held a full-time professional position since September 2015. I am currently working twenty-five to thirty hours per week as a cashier at Whole Foods Market. I still apply for full-time jobs in my field posted on LinkedIn, on company websites, and through contacts. I submit project proposals for consideration too. I'm even working on a business idea, though with some ambivalence. Do I really want to start a business at my age?

I am also prepping my house—where my children grew up and where my wife and I have lived for twenty-three years—for sale. And I am dealing with financial stress and the impact of years of unemployment on my marriage. I try to compartmentalize these different things so I don't fall apart or become deeply depressed. I push myself to remain optimistic and continue to look for ways to improve my situation.

What's challenging is holding on to all these pieces—the elements of my daily life—and, at the same time, maintaining my sense of self, the value I have to offer, all the "good" in my life and the love that's around me.

It's not easy.

When I first started working at Whole Foods, I dreaded running into someone I knew: a friend, a former colleague, a neighbor, a parent of one of my children's friends. I was embarrassed to be wearing a Whole Foods employee apron and name badge or to be seen bagging groceries or working a register.

I never avoided anyone, though. I always said hello, steadied myself, and had the conversation. I admit there were instances when one or the other of us turned away and I could feel myself getting emotional and holding back tears.

I never expected to land here.

I am well educated: Ivy League degree and an MBA from a top-tier business school. I have held senior marketing and client services positions at places like Fidelity, global ad agencies, and database marketing companies.

Yet, at this point in my life, I am a cashier making $12.60 per hour. I have come to realize that in the same way I was not defined by my senior vice president title at Fidelity, neither am I defined by my cashier job at Whole Foods. Adopting this mindset did not come easy and it did not happen overnight.

But today I can honestly say that I get pleasure out of interacting with people who come to my register, cracking little jokes, finding out about their day, and even getting to know some customers on a more personal level. And I have no reservation asking about the kind of work they do and—if the moment seems right—letting them know about my situation and seeing if they'd be open to me contacting them or connecting on LinkedIn.

Obviously, there are days when I feel down and unmotivated. Day after day of rejection is hard to take: all the part-time and full-time job applications that go unacknowledged, that just disappear into a black hole. I admit there are periods when I just want something to come to me, to relieve me of having to push so hard all the time. I'm tired. When I lose focus, I try not to feel too guilty even if the feeling lasts a few days. I always get back at it, reenergizing myself to make another concerted push. I don't know what this approach costs me. I can only say that I hope it hasn't been too detrimental to my efforts.

I know I must continue fighting and not give up. I try not to take things personally. Anyone looking for a job in today's market must contend with résumé-scanning software and key-word searches to help HR professionals reduce hundreds, if not thousands, of applications to a manageable number. There's no way around that.

What I do take personally, as a sixty-two-year-old looking for a job, is ageism, a practice that until recently has gone unchallenged in corporate America.

There are, however, a few bright spots on the job prospect front. I have been encouraged by the recent press regarding corporate "relaunch" and career "reentry" programs focused not only on women wanting to return to the workforce after long absences but also on programs reaching out to men.

What has really helped me get through these tough days, months, and years is the love and support that I have from family and dear friends. Maybe that sounds corny, but it has made all the difference. My "inner circle" has been sensitive to my situation, supportive in the ways they can be, tough love and all.

My greatest joy and comfort are my three children. Whatever I have achieved or have yet to achieve professionally, I am most proud of them. So even though I don't know how things are going to unfold in my next chapter, I do believe I will be OK. I have many things for which I am grateful. All I have to do is look around me to know that things could be much worse. Here's what I have learned since landing here:

- We are not defined by our professions. Our sense of self and the value that we bring to all facets of our life define us.

- Look for joy and pleasure in what you may have thought were unimportant or meaningless interactions, activities, and challenges. You never know what may come of them.

- Practice compartmentalizing aspects of your daily life to allow you to focus on the tasks at hand. It will be easier to apply for a job, write a cover letter, or have an informational phone call if you can suspend thinking about bills that are due, stresses in a relationship, or how long it's been since you worked.

- If you haven't realized it, know that you are not alone in facing the challenges of unemployment, ageism, and the stress associated with it all. Though research shows that there is a shortage of qualified workers, companies and their HR teams haven't realized the value and impact that older professionals can make.

- Though there may not be a clear vision of how things are going to unfold and play out, give pause to be thankful for all that you have, whether it be good health, the love of children, or the strength of character and fortitude you don't realize you're exhibiting every day.

Opening Up to Possibility

Remember to do the "Top This" exercise and to have three minutes of silence.

Having to weigh every decision against its affordability strips things down to the basics. Each choice is a trade-off. Will you buy this or that or go here or there? One's priorities come into sharp focus. There is no mindless consumption. There is no excess.

- What are your criteria for making financial decisions? How are they evolving? Are you mainly in survival mode? If there's anything left after the bills are paid, what do you do with these funds?

- What were the money messages that you got from your family? If you have siblings, are you the only one facing financial challenges? How does your financial situation affect your family dynamic? And how does it affect you? For example, maybe you can no longer help with the $1,800 shortfall in your dad's assisted-living-care expenses. Or maybe you need your daughter to give you money so that you can feed your grandchildren when they visit.

- What guilty pleasures do you still indulge in? What impulse-purchase habits are you finding hard to break? Have you found unconventional ways to enjoy the things you miss the most, even if you can't do so with the same regularity as before? A couple I know saves money and indulges their "inner foodies" by routinely splitting restaurant entrées.

- So often we learn more about who we are from adversity and hard times than we do from easy comfort. What have you learned about your own resilience? If you suddenly had lots of money, what lessons would you take with you from this period in your life?

- What steps are you taking to build meaning in your life? How might you begin this process? About a year ago I began meeting with a friend every Saturday morning for coffee. We go to a little neighborhood café and sit for a couple of hours, checking in with and being present for each other. I love this simple ritual and have come to see it as one of the highlights of my week.

• What illusions of control have you had to relinquish? You know the drill. You're pushing hard, ignoring signs, and willing things to happen to no avail. How do you know when you need to pause before taking the next step?

• What are you getting out of all of that bitching and moaning about where you've landed? How does it actually benefit you? Because complaining takes energy, it feels like action. Being stuck in a story can make you feel like you're actually doing something about it. But talking about it is not the same as doing something about it. Is there such a thing as complaining in a healthy way about an outcome that you're unhappy about? How do you know when you've gone over the line? At what point does all of that bellyaching become unproductive?

Chapter 7

Circling the Drain

You've got to know how to hustle and hang.

—Juan

You never drank $12 glasses of Chardonnay or used valet parking. You don't know those people and don't want to know them. You haven't worked steadily in two years, maybe longer. You're beat-up. Shell-shocked. Weary to the bone. You're juggling paying your utilities and buying your prescription meds. You scraped together this month's rent, but next month will be dicey—beyond dicey. You're only one payment behind on your car. They won't repossess it for that. Thank God. A nice account rep agreed to payment arrangements for your mobile phone. You know your ass is showing if your phone gets turned off. The last letter from the IRS was certified. You need a payment arrangement for your payment arrangement. You still owe your sister from the last time you borrowed money from her. You're so close to the edge, you hope you won't kick the pebble that launches the rock slide.

Clawing Your Way Back

When you've landed here, what's the play? When nothing works anymore, what do you do? When you've forgotten who you are and what you know, where do you begin?

You start with the tiniest step. Life is a series of choices. Each day you are presented with hundreds of opportunities to act or not act. You make choices. You choose. Clawing your way back is choosing to do a little more each day.

Depending on how bad things are, starting might just look like brushing your teeth and washing your face. That's all. Or maybe you put on clean clothes. You shave. Or you wash the dishes in the sink and do nothing more.

And if those steps are too big, start smaller.

It's shocking to be here. I know.

It never occurred to you that no one would hire you or that you'd be stuck in some low-wage job you hate. You've never had trouble landing a job before. Now getting arrested might be easier than getting an interview.

Once you hit fifty, even if you have a job, there just aren't that many opportunities for advancement. You know they're just looking for an opportunity to give you a package and boot you out the door. I just keep my head down and don't make waves.

—Joshua

Colleagues who could help you don't lift a finger. Your anger gives way to resignation and loss. There is this slow-motion dawning that the career you had is over. While you may still hold out hope for a job like the one you left, you know—and deep down you do know—that the longer you're unemployed, the more unlikely that will be.

After sending fifty—or maybe it's one hundred—job applications without getting a response, you start to question everything.

Some of you have shared staying in this limbo place for a long time, with sadness and loss tipping into depression.

I am sitting at my volunteer gig, where I am training in retail, and fighting back tears . . . I've cut everything that can possibly be cut from my budget. I have finally accepted that I have to sell my home and move into low-income housing. I am forty-nine.

—Tracy

Feelings of failure are overwhelming and everyone around you blames you. There is no understanding that the world has changed. Having a job does not mean you can pay the rent and feed yourself. No one acknowledges this.

—Mathew

Making sense out of all of this is a process. There will be good days and some very bad ones. It's disconcerting to be suddenly on the outside looking in at "normal" with your face pressed up against the window. You will feel unmoored if you've always belonged and your sense of who you are is tied up in your job title. And now there is no job title and no job.

The lack of responses to my valiant job-seeking effort is surprising to those who know me. If only I could live off a stipend of unsolicited, random praise like "There's no one with your experience" and "There's no one more hardworking, creative, resourceful, or talented than you." But, alas, with two children in college, accolades won't pay the tuition.

—Sarah

Here's what I know after talking to lots of people: the only way through this is through it. There's no cutting across the grass.

Being part of a community can help. Find a tribe. Your Resilience Circle is a place where you can confide in others who are on the same road. It gives you an opportunity to get out of your head and away from all that negative self-talk that's wearing you down. Being heard by people who are facing what you're facing can also lessen your feelings of isolation.

And if you're in an emotional free fall, your Resilience Circle can help you get your bearings and take those first few steps back from the abyss.

It's a beginning to build upon.

Grieving Versus Wallowing

Now, wallowing is different from grieving. Wallowing is giving up, feeling sorry for yourself, retreating into fear and isolation, and calling it "practicality."

Wallowing is a "stuck story." It's forfeiting your ability to choose the next step and your power to take action.

When you're grieving, denial can turn into just enough anger to spur healing actions, which are small steps that grow along a continuum. Making your bed one day can turn into making it every day. Willing yourself to get out of your sweat pants to meet with a friend for coffee can turn into a standing appointment every week.

The "Awfulizing" Trap

Wallowing can also lead you to "awfulize," or to take minor setbacks and to extrapolate them to awful extremes. Let's say you're not called back after a great interview. Awfulizing is thinking that your previous employer bad-mouthed you, that your reputation is ruined, that you will never work again, that you will lose your house, and that your spouse will divorce you.

Awfulizing puts the worst spin on things. It has you shadowboxing with a future that hasn't happened and likely won't happen. It's a true parade of horribles. If you're not vigilant, awfulizing can get you really worked up—and the next thing you know, you'll be tense and upset about events in some imaginary future.

Awfulizing is natural, so it helps to have safeguards against it.

A partner or a trusted friend can help you avoid the awfulizing trap, but as your awareness sharpens, you will recognize when you're in its grip.

Taking Care of Your Shell

Going through all of this takes such a toll on your health. I woke up one morning and heard someone screaming and realized it was me.

—Karen

When you're circling the drain, you let things go, and your appearance, health, and well-being are often first.

You can't afford your gym membership, so you stop exercising. You don't feel like cooking, so you eat fast food or cold cereal for dinner. You put off your hair appointments, and it shows.

I'm sixty-one years old and washed-up. I only wish I could fake normal.

—Deborah

You're "tore up from the floor up," rotating between two T-shirts and a pair of worn-out sweat pants.

You get the picture.

You're kidding yourself if you think that looking worn down at the heels doesn't affect your outlook and mind-set. How will you even begin to get yourself back if every time you look in the mirror and at your surroundings, you're filled with self-loathing and disgust?

It's hard to choose yourself when you've been knocked down so many times that you barely care anymore.

You're in a fight. If you don't show up for yourself and plant a flag somewhere, who is going to?

Looking at Your Own Stuff

We have to walk all of the way around the board and look at our own issues too.

For the last seven months you've been living for free in your neat-freak brother's spare bedroom. You don't even make an effort to keep the room together, and you know it's pissing him off. The room's a wreck, with your clothes strewn across the floor and dirty dishes piled high. You haven't made the bed once since you got there. Your brother comes home from work and finds you propped up in the easy chair, watching TV. And you're fifty-two, not twenty-two.

At a minimum, *you* don't need the extra tension that this situation will cause—especially not with everything else that's wearing you down.

Part of clawing our way back is showing gratitude for those things, however small, that are going our way. And having a free, safe place to live is a gift, not a given.

Excuses, Excuses, Excuses

You'll think of a million reasons why you can't get started. And they'll be good, inventive, thoughtful reasons. You'll impress yourself.

But who are you shortchanging? You.

Working out once a week is a good way to start, if you haven't already been doing that. Or simply just get out and walk.

And if that's still too much, break your walk down into smaller chunks. The point is to move your body and to do what you can to stay fit. How you choose to do that doesn't really matter. Just start somewhere and build.

The same idea goes for food. If you start looking emaciated and feeling like a scarecrow or packing on the pounds and feeling like the Pillsbury Doughboy, you're not going to be happy—especially if you berate yourself about it. You're just going to feel worse than you already do.

I won't hit you over the head with the importance of diet and exercise to your overall health. You know about that already.

But here's something to think about: because of our financial situations, a large number of us are planning to work well into our sixties and seventies. But poor health may get in the way of that.

According to AARP, "more than 70 million older adults ages 50 and older suffer from at least one chronic condition, and 11 million live with five or more chronic conditions."[1]

So four out of five of us are living with health ailments that could potentially limit our daily activities, physical functions, and independence. But these health ailments can also limit our ability to work.

The big four—cancer, strokes, heart disease, and diabetes—account for two-thirds of all deaths in the United States. Obviously we can't dodge every bullet. Some medical conditions are just in our genes and the luck of the draw. But better outcomes are tied to early detection, preventative care, and how well we take care of ourselves. If we can stave off—or at least better manage—some of the chronic conditions that could force us to give up our independence too soon, we should.

Taking Care of Your Crib

You may no longer notice the disorder in your living space, but it assaults your spirit every time you walk in the front door. All of that stuff is draining your energy.

You pay a price for the stacked papers, the unopened mail, and the dirty dishes. You lose a little bit of yourself every time you step over those jumbled power cords or that pile of unwashed clothes.

The last thing you need is for the upheaval that you feel on the inside to be mirrored in your living space. Lord knows, you don't need another thing to feel bad about.

So start somewhere, and do something—anything. Clear the surfaces in the room where you spend the most time.

Only you can decide to stop making excuses and to start showing up for yourself. Only you will know when you're sick and tired of being sick and tired and truly want a different outcome.

Getting through the lowest points is all about deciding not to stay trapped and choiceless. It's about recognizing that you can make choices and that your actions matter more than your words.

Author Marilyn Paul sums it up perfectly in her book *It's Hard to Make a Difference When You Can't Find Your Keys: The Seven-Step Path to Becoming Truly Organized.* Mired in our possessions and wallowing in self-pity, we deny the world our talents, our gifts, and our hearts.

We also deny ourselves the opportunity to choose more meaningful and satisfying lives. That's why we need to work through our grief. That's why we need to take care of our shells and to bring order to our homes. It's how we claw our way back.

Your Tax Dollars at Work and Other Support

But sometimes it's not a question of choice. You just can't. Things have become so dire, so on edge, that you're scrambling just to keep a roof over your head and food on the table. You can't focus on anything else; you can't focus on your grief or on the disorder that surrounds you. You need immediate stopgap assistance to function, to live.

The government offers some limited help, although lawmakers are shredding existing safety-net programs across the country. Cuts are getting more draconian, not less.

The programs described below will not pull you out of a deep hole. If you're in a financial free fall, the most they will do is slow your descent. But in some instances that little bit of breathing room will be enough for you to regain your footing to go another round.

Most people who lose their jobs have no qualms about applying for unemployment benefits. But applying for food stamps, Medicaid, energy assistance, or other safety-net programs gives them pause. There is a stigma and shame attached to applying to them. Many think of these programs as "welfare," and, whoa . . . that's something altogether different.

Get over it. Haven't you paid into the system? Don't your tax dollars fund these programs? Don't be ridiculous. Get the support you need.

For help with housing, call the HOPE Hotline at the Homeownership Preservation Foundation. The number is 1-888-995-HOPE (4673), and its website is https://995hope.org/.

If you own your home and are behind in your mortgage payments and struggling to make them on time or trying to avoid foreclosure, you can get assistance from the HOPE Hotline.

The Homeownership Preservation Foundation offers several different programs, depending on your circumstances and on the kind of help you need. When you call, an intake officer will take your basic information and determine what kind of assistance you might qualify for, and then he or she will set you up with a housing counselor. There are, of course, eligibility criteria that you must meet to qualify for the programs.

For example, in some cases you must still be receiving unemployment benefits to qualify. In others, your eligibility might hinge on whether your mortgage company is participating in a particular program. Of course, not everyone can be helped, but Homeownership Preservation Foundation housing counselors totally "get" how dire your situation is and will work with you to try to find a mortgage assistance program that fits your circumstances.

But don't wait until you're months behind on your mortgage. Call as soon as you know you're in trouble. These programs can take time to go into effect. And the last thing you want to hear is that you could have been helped but you waited too long.

If you are sixty-two and cash poor but have a lot of equity in your home, the National Council on Aging (NCOA) (https://www.ncoa.org /economic-security/home-equity/) can help you explore the pros and cons of reverse mortgages.

Don't forget about your options for finding housemates.

You're cringing. You don't want a housemate. You need your privacy. You like your solitude. You don't want a stranger in your house. It's dangerous, and so on and so on.

I know. *I know.* I've been there.

But here's the deal: in the new normal of financial insecurity, all of us will have to learn to think strategically, to use the assets we have, and to hustle and hang. If a roommate is going to bring in some cash and help save your butt, you need to consider getting one.

So, if you're struggling to make your house payments or your rent, think about how much easier it would be if you were divvying up your expenses. Think strategically. Think about utilizing all of your assets. Do what you need to do.

Sara's Homestay (https://www.sarahomestay.com/homestay) provides rooms and meals to foreign students and lists about ten thousand hosts around the world. If you have one or more spare bedrooms and would be willing to host one or more foreign students, this resource might work for you. There will be a greater demand for your residence if you live in a popular city near local amenities and have access to public transportation. Students are guaranteed a continental breakfast, dinner, and a modest, clean room and a bathroom, both of which may be shared with another student.

A friend has been hosting one or two students on a regular basis through this program and speaks very highly of it. While the cooking part would kill me, she says that she just makes a little more of whatever she's eating herself and that it's no big deal.

There are a number of additional housing resources, including home sharing, listed in Chapter 11.

Many of you who are facing financial hardships may not know that you're eligible for the federal government's Supplemental Nutrition Assistance Program, or SNAP. SNAP, formerly known as food stamps, helps low-income seniors buy food. But many boomer-aged Americans who would qualify for the program don't participate in it. Please consult the following websites for more information: http://www.fns.usda.gov/snap/apply and http://www.fns.usda.gov/snap/snap-special-rules-elderly-or-disabled.

For additional assistance, you may wish to check out the National Council on Aging's (NCOA) Senior Snap Enrollment Initiative, a national program that "supports efforts by community-based organizations and agencies to assist (adults age sixty and over) in applying

and enrolling in SNAP": https://www.ncoa.org/economic-security
/benefits/food-and-nutrition/senior-hunger-snap/.

*Last year I finally took food stamps. I was embarrassed to take
them. I was raised not to take charity. Even though I know my
tax dollars help pay for them, I'm still not entirely comfortable
with them.*

—Chris

According to AARP, only about one-third of adults age sixty and
above who are eligible for SNAP benefits actually receive them.

*A lot of people who need food stamps and qualify for them are
too ashamed to get them. Don't be silly. Government programs
are there as a hand up.*

—Zoe

There are a lot of reasons for the lack of participation. One is the
stigma attached to it—the feeling that food stamps are for *"those* people" and *not you*. That is especially true if you are someone who's had
career-choice privilege and big jobs and made decent money. Coming
to terms with the fact that you actually need food stamps right now to
make ends meet is going to be hard for you to wrap your brain around.

*You have to process the whole food stamps experience differ-
ently. Stop seeing using food stamps as failure. Look at it as
strategy—a temporary fix to get you up on your feet again.
Nothing more and nothing less.*

—Zoe

The process of applying for SNAP benefits can also be demeaning.
The wait is long and the questions are intrusive. People interviewed
for this book reported feeling invisible or fearing being treated like
second-class citizens during the enrollment process.

Get down there early. If the office opens at eight in the morning, be there by seven at the latest. The lines are long. Be prepared to wait for hours for your name to be called.

—Juan

Some people complain that the SNAP benefit amounts are too low to justify all of the hassle. But think of it this way: when you're down to your last bit of cash, not having to spend it on food means that you can take care of other necessities, like putting a little gas in your car or keeping your mobile phone turned on.

The intake officer sitting across from you may only have one teaspoon of power, but he wields it over you and can totally eff you up. It is tempting to be chatty. Just answer the questions you're asked. Be polite and don't flex. Now is not the time for your lecture on how the intake process could be streamlined.

—Dan

So, how much money does the SNAP benefit give you? That depends on your income and on the size of your household. Do note that, for purposes of eligibility, your house is not counted, but your vehicle may count as a resource for SNAP purposes under certain conditions. So check the rules. For the fiscal year 2018, the maximum amount for a one-person household is $192 per month, and the maximum amount for a two-person household is $352.

I was in the food stamps waiting room and left to go to the bathroom. I was surprised by how absolutely pristine it was. When I came back to the waiting area, a Hispanic woman asked to see my intake ticket. She was worried I might have been called while I was away. No one went to the bathroom, because they didn't want to lose their places in line.

—Kelly

Most SNAP rules apply to all households, but there are exceptions. For example, persons fifty and older are exempt from the SNAP work requirement. SNAP requires all Able-bodied Adults Without Dependents (ABAWD) ages eighteen to forty-nine and not disabled "to work at least 80 hours per month, participate in qualifying education and training activities at least 80 hours per month, or comply with a workforce program."[2]

If you are fifty or over, none of that applies to you.

SNAP "money" is deposited on a plastic EBT (electronic benefits transfer card) that works much like a debit card. You can use your card in grocery stores and at other approved retailers, including farmers' markets, to buy food and food-related items, like seeds and plants to grow food. You cannot buy hot food. And you can't buy pet food, vitamins, or household products like toothpaste, paper towels, or dish detergent—and, of course, you can't buy alcohol or tobacco products.

The first time I used my food stamp card, I drove to a grocery store across town away from my neighborhood. I held my breath when I swiped the card, afraid it would not work and I'd be left standing there looking foolish. I avoided the cashier's eyes, too. But the card worked, and the cashier did not seem to notice me or even care.

—Owen

Statistics show that if you are over fifty and unemployed, the duration of your unemployment is going to be substantially longer than that of your younger counterparts. That means that it could last for months if not years. With no income, you will be hemorrhaging cash. It can get very dicey very fast.

SNAP is one of the very few safety-net programs for older adults without young children. Many of us boomers are in limbo land, too young for Medicare and social security and ineligible for programs designed for households with children under eighteen.

I am running up all this debt using my plastic safety net, my Visa card.

—Andy

SNAP benefits may not be a lot, but they are a good stopgap measure when you're circling the drain and need to conserve your cash. And in truly dire situations, SNAP will be your first line of defense against hunger.

So please stop beating up on yourself. If you think SNAP can help you, at least go down to your local office and see if you're eligible for it.

And one last thing, if you're wondering how on earth you will eat well on $4 per day, check out Leanne Brown's *Good and Cheap* book and website. It's a labor of love she created for people on tight budgets. She gives away one cookbook for every one purchased. The recipes I've tried are delicious and straightforward. You can read more about Leanne here: https://www.leannebrown.com/about.

There are also programs that can help you heat and cool your home. You can call the Low-Income Home Energy Assistance Program at 1-866-674-6327. Also consult the following websites for more information: http://www.acf.hhs.gov/programs/ocs/program/liheap/about and http://www.acf.hhs.gov/programs/ocs/liheap-state-and-territory-contact-listing.

You know the drill. You're relieved when the weekend comes, because utility companies typically don't disconnect services for nonpayment on Saturdays and Sundays. You're praying for snow in June, because you know that your water and energy are safe in freezing weather. You walk in the front door holding your breath, immediately flip the light switch, relieved, once again, that your lights are still on.

You don't have to live like this. You can get help. LIHEAP is a federally funded program that helps low-income families manage their energy costs. LIHEAP helps with energy-bill payments, energy-crisis assistance, utility shutoff prevention, weatherization, and minor energy-related home repairs.

Consult the LIHEAP website to learn more about the program and how to apply.

Again, think strategically. Programs like LIHEAP were designed for people facing temporary hardships. Ditch the shame. Do what you need to do to secure yourself.

Chris Hawkins at seniorliving.org has put together a good list of additional resources to help older adults who are short on cash with housing, health care, transportation, and more: http://www.senior living.org/retirement/resources-surviving-social-security/.

And one of my favorite help tools is the National Council on Aging's BenefitsCheckUp. You fill out a form online with basic information and it literally scours some 2,500 benefit programs across the country to see which ones you might qualify for. The programs cover food, rent, transportation, and medication: https://www.benefitscheckup.org.

Meet Juan

"Get off the throne," sixty-five-year-old Juan said as she sipped her bottled water. "These people are struggling and turning down seventy-thousand-dollar jobs because they're used to making a hundred and forty thousand. It just doesn't make sense."

Juan was referring to some boomer-aged friends who'd formerly been high earners but were facing tough times after losing their jobs and were still in denial.

Juan admitted that being alone was a powerful motivator. "I have no backup. If it's going to happen, I have to make it happen."

Juan's approach to work is that money is green. She's always working multiple jobs as part of Minding Your Business, the company she started ten years ago because she'd always wanted to be an entrepreneur.

A few months back she asked me whether I wanted to work with her on an "organization" contract she'd won. I thought that maybe she meant community organizing along the lines of what Barack Obama had done in Chicago. What Juan meant was organizing somebody's closet.

No way was I doing that. "Get off your throne," she said.

The time before that, Juan was rushing off to make sure a client's driveway was cleared of snow before she returned home from a Paris business trip. And before that she'd had a gig as a secret shopper.

"You do what you have to do," she said. "Money from these small gigs adds up."

Pink Slip

Six years ago Juan lost her job as a program manager after ten years in the position. She admitted that she'd hoped that she'd be spared from the layoffs but that when she looked back on it, she could see the signs that her days had been numbered. The pink slip had not entirely been a surprise.

For the first few days after being laid off, Juan slept late, prepared "good" breakfasts, organized her home, and just rested: "I had a little cash set aside and was owed my vacation days, so I wasn't totally broke."

Then she got busy.

She didn't have time to grieve. "That's just not me," she said. She got herself together and went down to the Department of Aging. She brought home its resource guide and spent the next two weeks studying it.

"Every morning I'd get up and sit in the same spot on my couch, devouring that book." She knew it backward and forward.

No Shame

Juan is not the kind of person who's afraid to ask for help. Many people facing the reality of downward mobility are in hiding. Not Juan. "You can't hide," she said. "You've got to let somebody know what's happening to you."

Juan asks for help, but she offers it too. She's not a "got mine"–type person who's always pulling up the drawbridge behind her. Juan keeps her heel in the door, holding it open for the folks pulling up the rear. She is literally a walking resource guide.

When I needed help making my mortgage payment, it was Juan who told me about the program that had helped her, and I got the temporary support I needed. She told me which days seniors could go to the YMCA for free and taught me how to use vouchers to get free fresh fruit and vegetables from the farmers' markets around town, in case I ever needed that.

Juan's not ashamed or embarrassed about her situation, either. "Why should I be?" she asked, incredulous that anyone would be embarrassed.

When she can't afford the luxuries she was accustomed to—expensive restaurants, weekend getaways, and the latest fashions—she just tells herself, *This too shall pass.* She's adjusted to the situation. "Removing myself from the throne was not easy, but after a while I didn't miss all of that stuff. Been there, done that. It was time to open up new doors," she said.

The New Normal

What Juan misses most from her old life is spontaneous travel, especially to her hometown in West Virginia. "And don't forget a nice bottle of wine with some Chilean sea bass," she added. For her, pure luxury meant getting her nails done once a week. But none of that is in the budget anymore.

It's not that she's given up everything. Juan's just much more careful now about where and how she spends her money. There are no impulse purchases or indulgence buying.

"I don't shop as much anymore," she said. "I go shopping in my closet." Luckily she entered this chapter of her life with a fabulous wardrobe.

Juan is focused on the future. She's teaching an introduction-to-computer-technology class to "seniors" at a local university. Working with them is giving her a sobering look at her own future and the effect of health challenges on quality of life.

"I am not focused on today," she said. "I am focused on how I want to land, in five and ten years from now," she said.

Twenty-five years ago, she bought a house for about $50,000 in what was then a marginal and undesirable neighborhood in Washington, DC. She recalled that her credit was "OK" in those days and that her mortgage's interest rate was through the roof at 12 percent.

Hanging on to that house is her top priority, and she'll do it "no matter what." That house is her security and her safety net.

She's taken in boarders a few times to help with the house payments, but that didn't work for her. "They always disappear when the money is due or want to make partial payments." It wasn't worth the trouble.

"Besides they started bringing me *their* personal problems to deal with . . . I didn't need that."

Juan is meticulous and pays her bills ahead of time when she can. "I stay on top of my bills. The equity in my house and a high credit score give me options."

Her plan is to continue working for as long she can. She has just applied for social security and is working part-time in a corporate office three days a week. It's not too far from where I live, and the bus ride is only eighty-five cents. Sometimes she treats herself to an Uber ride if it's raining or too hot outside.

Juan hasn't decided where she'll go after selling her home, but she thinks she'll stay in the DC area. "DC offers more benefits for seniors than other cities," she said. "I know I'll be OK."

Here are Juan's rules for life in the new normal:

- Money is green. Get off your throne. Stop turning your nose up at small jobs. The income adds up.

- Don't have a pity party. That's hard if you're used to living better. Allow yourself a really good cry now and then and a nice glass of something that you like to drink. But keep moving.

- Find out which government programs you're eligible for, and apply to them.

- If you still have good credit, do everything you can do to keep it.

Stepping Back from the Abyss

Remember to do the "Top This" exercise and to have three minutes of silence.

Clawing your way back is about starting somewhere. It's about taking that first step, however small or tentative. It's about continuing when you don't feel like it. It's knowing ahead of time that there will be times when you'll fall off the wagon and relapse into frustration, numbness, and even despair. It happens to everyone on this path. Expect it. But as you gain more coping skills and strategizing tools, you'll cycle through that craziness faster. You'll pick yourself up and keep on trekking.

- Who are you talking to about what's going on with you? Who do you need to hear from? If you're not talking to anyone, how are you managing your stress? How are you taking care of your body?

- In what parts of your life are you your own agent? Where and when have you gone to bat for yourself? Where are you staying quiet when you need to speak up?

- What is your worst fear—your personal parade of horribles? How do you break out of awfulizing? How do you catch yourself before you are in full reaction mode to some imaginary future?

- What should you be facing that you're not facing? What's just not doable anymore? Are you ready now to come out of denial? Is it that the rent you're paying is too high, or is it the mortgage? Should you really be thinking about moving into a smaller place or getting a boarder? Should you be ditching your car or trading it in for something smaller? Should you be thinking about moving in with a family member? Are you going to have to take a job way beneath your skill level to make ends meet? Or maybe you should be joining a food co-op to cut expenses. What are you ready to face—or consider now—that you weren't ready to face before?

- Cash poor, we're going to have to get "old-school" and inventive about identifying resources and looking at our options. For example, if you need to move, you likely don't have the resources to just call up ABC Moving Company and arrange for "fast, stress-free service." I'm one of five women on "moving duty" this weekend for a mutual friend who's relocating from a two-bedroom to a one-bedroom apartment in her building. She's supplying the munchies, the wine, and the moving dollies. We're hauling the boxes into the elevator and up to her new place. Male friends and relatives are moving the bigger furniture. How have you had to use old-school or unconventional approaches to get something done?

◆ What's your experience of asking for help—real help; the kind that could be perceived as an inconvenience to the person you're asking? When's the last time you offered that level of assistance? Most of us are not going to be able to pay for all the services we need. We are not going to be able to manage the next twenty to thirty years alone. We're going to need help—a lot of it—and we're going to have to offer help—a lot of it.

◆ I've listed some federally sponsored safety-net programs in this book. But your community may have additional city- or state-sponsored initiatives that help older adults. If there is no hard-copy brochure, each person can download his or her own copy and read it from front to back. Senior Care (http://www.seniorcare.com/) has a comprehensive list (scroll down on the home page) of resource guides for seniors in all fifty states but not Washington, DC. Find a list of resources for those in Washington, DC, here: http://dcoa .dc.gov/.

◆ There are also private-sector incentive programs for seniors. For example, my neighborhood's grocery chain, Harris Teeter, offers a 5 percent discount on purchases to seniors sixty and older every Thursday. That's just one such program. There are a lot of them. For example, here's a list of senior discounts on restaurants: https://www.these niorlist.com/senior-discounts/list-of-senior-discounts-restaurants/ and retail stores https://www.theseniorlist.com/senior-discounts/ senior-discounts-retail-apparel/. On the same website, you will find additional senior discount lists for grocery stores, prescriptions, and travel.

Chapter 8

Borrowing Money from Family and Friends

I have been hiding in plain sight for years. Trying to appear normal is exhausting. I think one or two of my friends suspect that things aren't as I pretend they are but don't know how to ask if I am OK. And honestly, I don't know if I'd be willing to talk about it with them.

—Marcy

At some point on this journey, you will likely need to borrow money from family and friends (or have them borrow money from you). You will be as surprised by those who do help you as you will be by those who don't.

But here's the deal and what you have to let sink in: no one owes you anything. No one is under any obligation whatsoever to help you . . . not your aging parents; your siblings; your adult children, nieces, or nephews; or your closest friends.

I don't care what you've done for them in the past. I don't care how many times you bailed out so-and-so. I don't care how much love and attention you showered on whomever. You did what you did because you wanted to, and there is no requirement that anyone return the favor.

Are you still with me? This can be the hardest pill to swallow. And for it to sink in, you're going to have to circle back to this point over and over again.

But do what you must to wrap your brain around this concept, because if you don't, you'll be setting yourself up for a lot of disappointment.

It's Not That No One Helps

When I lost my job three years ago, one friend in particular proved to be my touchstone and sanity refuge. We must have borrowed the same $300 from each other a dozen times. We might have been splitting peanuts, but when she had money, I had money, and vice versa.

Our friendship was one of the very few places I could go without feeling that I had to fake normal. Dispensing all of those cheery little "I'm fine" responses when someone asks how you are gets exhausting.

This friend, a very few others, and my mother and daughter form the scaffolding that has held me up. I always knew my mother and daughter would not let me go over the railing no matter what.

But what I've learned from you is not all families help.

At fifty-five, I asked my seventy-eight-year-old dad if I could move back home temporarily, and he told me no and that he had never heard of someone my age moving back in with their parents.

—Christina

I am living on fumes after my divorce. My two brothers are doing quite well. I am the sole caretaker of our mother, who has dementia. My brothers hired a senior-care manager to make sure I was not spending money on myself. One drives down from New York City to take her to lunch once a month, but that's it. Everything else falls on me. Proceeds from the family house are to be shared equally among us. I asked my brothers if I could have the house, because they don't need the money. They wouldn't even consider it. They think it's my fault that I'm here and forget their own drama and the help they received when they fell on hard times.

—Allison

My eighty-six-year-old mother looks at me like what happened is all my fault. She has no sympathy whatsoever. I wouldn't believe it myself if it weren't happening to me.

—Sarah

Not Asking for Help When You Need It

A lot of us grew up believing that you don't tell people your problems. You handle things yourself.

—Stanley

If you grew up learning to "handle things yourself," your "fake" might be so good that no one even knows you're in trouble. Some friends and family may put it together that you haven't been working steadily and are probably out of money by now. But lots of people just aren't paying that close attention.

They're just not going to dig that deep if you seem fine on the surface. They may not notice that you're ordering appetizers when everyone else is ordering entrées, that you're "filling up" your SUV with seven dollars' worth of gas, or that you replace things only when they're falling apart.

But faking normal can cost you too. You may be so good at it that your friends don't know to tell you about things that could actually help you out of your situation, like that job opportunity with your name on it or that deal on a more affordable apartment.

A minister friend once said to me that God works through people. He cannot begin to help you if you don't let folks know what's going on with you.

That friend who'd be willing to help you cover the shortfall on your rent can't step in if he doesn't even know that you're in trouble.

There are, of course, risks involved with coming clean. You open your kimono, ask for help, and there it is: that blank stare and loss of respect.

It happens. We've all been there.

While it may be true that you don't talk to people about how bad it is, I've found that people don't want to know. After a while they stop asking you to go out, because you always say no. My family doesn't know, and they don't want to know. People don't want to be bothered with your problems. The stress adds up to health problems that add to the stress. It's a vicious circle. The life I live is a secret, but that's not because I want it that way.

—Deb

Borrowing and Lending Money

Many of you have expressed dismay when friends and family haven't helped you, especially if you've been there for them. I have learned that some people don't lend others money as a matter of principle. They've just been burned too many times.

I'd rather "give" a friend a lesser amount than lend a lot and have that hanging in the air every time we see each other.

—Edward

And it is true that there are borrowers who treat loans as "gifts with nagging attached."

There's the big sob story, and you fork over some cash and then have to chase them for it. One friend took his two daughters to Paris a few months after borrowing a substantial sum from me. Four years later, I still have not been paid back.

—Andy

I let a friend's brother stay in my house for one year without paying rent. I kicked him out after he turned up one day with a new car.

—Joyce

On the flip side, if you're wondering why people you know, including family members, don't come to you for help, here's why:

Nothing blows a colder wind through a friendship (even a very close one) than the request for money.

—Elizabeth

You don't want to do it. You've always taken care of yourself and always been able to pull yourself out of fixes. What's happening now is new terrain.

—Marc

Even if I took a loan from a friend or family member, I'm not sure how or when I could repay it. Things are that precarious. I'm conflicted. I need help but don't want to ask.

—Deborah

Friends Who Leave You Hanging

If you're wondering why some good friends give you a cold shoulder, getting burned in the past probably has something to do with it.

But that's not the only reason that friends and family don't help when asked to do so.

Many are just not in a position to do anything. They're financially strapped themselves and are dealing with their own health challenges or with those of their aging parents, or they're managing nightmare scenarios with siblings and grandchildren who have gone off the rails.

And some folks who look like they could help are faking normal themselves. They're barely hanging on, mortgaged to the hilt. All of those outer trappings are the biggest fake-outs of all.

But some who you suspect—scratch that: you *know*—could help don't for reasons that have nothing to do with being burned. And you learn things about your friendships with them that you didn't actually want to know. You learn that they have outer boundaries.

That outer boundary could be a $500 loan or a $1,500 loan. It could be asking to crash at a friend's place for a few weeks or a few months. It could be asking someone to make a call on your behalf or to introduce you to a new job prospect. Whatever the question is, the answer is no. You have hit that point beyond which your friend will not go.

And it will rock you.

You will think about all of your years together and the decades you spent with each other, dealing with marriages, divorces, children, the deaths of parents, medical diagnoses, and addictions. And yet, here is the bright line in the sand.

But here's the hard part: *they* owe you nothing for what you've done for them. Whatever you did, you did because you wanted to— you did because of who you are.

It is discomfiting to learn that someone so dear to you would walk away and let you just sail over a cliff.

It's hard to know what to do with that and how to hold it. How are you supposed to interact with that person now?

There are no easy answers here. Every situation has a million unique details. Some friendships will be irrevocably altered, and you will both know it. With others, the shift will be so subtle that the friend may not notice it. But you will never look at him or her in quite the same way.

You will get through it. Millions of us have. It's just part of the journey.

Support from a Most Unlikely Source

I'm sharing this story to give you an example of receiving help from someone you'd never expect to receive it from. It's about a loan I got from my friend Elijah.

Elijah is not your average guy.

He is barefoot and shirtless always, dressed only in jean shorts cut high on the side like a loincloth, exposing his toned, fit legs.

He's also beautiful, the color of caramel candy. At seventy years old, he stands easily over six feet tall. A white-gray beard frames his face, and ropy locks of the same color hang down his back.

He's a fixture in my neighborhood. I have seen him around for years and, until about three years ago, always from the safe distance of my car: high-arched feet, toes splayed out and leather-like, seemingly immune to the hot summer pavement.

Our paths crossed one Sunday at a drumming circle in a park near my home.

While speaking with him, I learned that he's not homeless. For the last three years he's lived in a small single-room apartment with a small cookstove, a refrigerator, and a bathroom. And before that he lived as a "nomad" on a religious quest, "houseless by choice," he says, for thirty-five years.

Friends have asked why I accepted his invitation for coffee. Curious, maybe. Intrigued, too, by his freedom from striving and my belief that wisdom, growth, and learning can come from anyone.

"How is this coffee thing going to work?" I asked, glancing at his semi-nudity and noticing for the first time that Elijah is missing most of his teeth. He slid a drawstring bag off his shoulder. The bag held a T-shirt and sandals, his entry uniform into the world where the rest of us reside.

We exchanged cell numbers. I suggested that we meet at Potter's House, a neighborhood café and "living room" with an eclectic clientele and a pay-what-you-can option on the menu.

Elijah and I have met there many, many times over the years, laughing and talking on each occasion for a couple of hours. When I was in crisis, he insisted on paying for my bowl of oatmeal, coffee, or carton of juice. "I know you're on a budget," he said after he learned that I wasn't working.

Elijah lives on $500 a month out of the $900 a month he gets in veteran's benefits. He told me that he spends $150 on subsidized rent,

$35 on his cell phone, $40 on his Internet hot-spot subscription, and the remaining $275 on electricity and food. "I don't spend any money on clothes," he said, laughing. Out of his $900 monthly income, he sets aside $400 each month in savings and has done so for years.

Our interactions are easy and effortless. Friends have expressed concern about my safety with a friend like Elijah. Others have worried that he might try to hit on me and that he could become a pest. But there is no "boy-girl" energy in our interactions at all. Mostly, I don't feel judged or sized up. Elijah has no interest in my education, my work history, or any of my props or credentials, for that matter.

Once he lent me $2,500 to get me through a particularly rough patch. "I keep a little to the side to help my friends caught up in the stuff world," he told me. It was not lost on me that Elijah had come through for me when others with significantly more means had not. It was deeply humbling. I thought about all of the times I could have done more for friends in need—could have been there in a more wholehearted way—and was not.

I felt shame around that.

Last Christmas I invited Elijah to dinner with my family. I knew I couldn't just turn up at the family gathering with Elijah. My eighty-six-year-old mother had to approve of him, and she did. To honor her, Elijah wore "normal" shorts, a shirt, and sandals. (I had suggested long pants, but they were out of the question!)

Occasionally, Elijah ventures "off of the grid" and into some unfamiliar mental space. "Elijah, I can't follow you there," I said when he told me that "shapeshifting" would one day regrow his teeth.

"I know. I know," he said, smiling. "One day you'll understand."

Early on, I asked him if a friendship with him required that I agree with him. "Of course not," he said, looking at me with those honest eyes, head tilted to the side.

From the astonished gazes of onlookers, I know that we make an odd pair walking down the street back to my car. Elijah always gives me a quick hug "heart to heart" before heading off, barefoot, to his "office" in the park near my house.

Resilience Circle Reflection

Two Sides to Every Story

Remember to do the "Top This" exercise and to have three minutes of silence.

It is very likely that your circle of family and friends will include people facing the same financial challenges you're facing, people doing worse than you, and people doing much, much better than you. You're going to be managing a potent cocktail of emotions as you navigate these various relationships. There's who you are and how you feel, and then there's the ideal self that you'd like to be. You're going to learn a lot about who you are through this process and a lot about other people too.

- With financial pressure comes a lot of worry and stress. You've told me that you want your friends and family to be able to express themselves and to share what's happening in their lives. You've also said that you're not always up to hearing about how fabulous their vacations were, about the details of their $40,000 kitchen remodels, or about how much money they've saved for retirement—especially when it's much more than you've saved. How do you continue to be a supportive friend while managing the (normal) pangs of envy that you may feel from time to time? How do you avoid leaking your frustration? How do you manage your desire to limit contact, avoid the relationship, or even exit it altogether? And how do you discern when a "friend" is innocently sharing the events of his or her life as opposed to flaunting his or her successes with the intent of making you feel bad about your own situation?

- Some friends and family are not going to hear you when you say that you can no longer afford to do X, Y, and Z. They're going to nod politely and then invite you to do X, Y, and Z over and over again. What do you think is behind their not hearing you? How do you respond to it?

- What are the politics of who you tell and who you don't tell about your financial challenges? And if you tell people about it, how much do you share?

◆ Some of you have reported that you do volunteer work and that it gives you a deep sense of gratification. You've said that when you're helping others, you don't feel so caught up in your own needs. How are you giving back? And if you're not, how might you begin?

Chapter 9

The Changing World of Work

We didn't plan for age discrimination and expulsion from the workforce ten years before retirement to strip us of our well-thought-out plans. We did the right thing. We were corporately loyal and honest and good neighbors, taxpayers, and citizens, and we put away money for rainy days and retirement. What we didn't see, and what's new, is this enforced and silent drowning. A generation of folks who were successful for most of their lives are now minimized in the twenty-first-century workforce, downsized and outsized into silent shame and poverty.

—Bruce

Major shifts in the global economy and rapid technological advances have transformed how business is done and fundamentally changed how we work, play, and live.

Freelancing Is in Our Futures, Like It or Not

To compete in the global marketplace, companies have to be nimble and agile. This need for flexibility is changing the future of work. Well-paid, secure jobs with health insurance and employer-matched retirement plans are being replaced by contract work and contingent, part-time/temporary, and freelance jobs.

Flexible staffing arrangements allow companies to expand and contract their staffs accordion-style based on their workloads. With no obligation to pay benefits or to provide offices, desks, computers, or filing cabinets, overhead for these companies is low.

Even how we define the workplace is changing dramatically. Remote-work technologies, ubiquitous Internet access, and cloud-based computing allow workers with in-demand skills to work independently across industries from anywhere in the world.

Just look at how WeWork, now valued by investors at about $20 billion since opening its doors in 2010, is changing the work landscape. Dubbed the "landlord to the gig economy," WeWork is part real estate, part technology, and part hospitality company. It may not be the biggest coworking company, but it's the leader in what has become a global movement. Today, WeWork serves clients in 212 coworking spaces in twenty countries around the world.[1]

Freelancers Union estimates that 57.3 million people, or about one in three US workers, are currently employer independent and part of the freelance contingent workforce.[2] This number is projected to increase by half or more over the next decade.

But even well-established, mature companies are looking for ways to create more engaging work. WeWork is not just attracting solopreneurs, tech start-ups, and early-stage businesses. Fully a quarter of its customers are corporate clients.

Millions of older Americans who are short on retirement savings are looking at working well into their sixties and seventies, health permitting, just to make ends meet. For many of us, accustomed to tenured positions and long service to a handful of employers, the new norm of contract work, with its unpredictable hours and earnings, is daunting and undesirable.

When outsourcing jobs became the norm, many of us were left in a constant state of struggle. We're too overqualified to get hired for the service jobs that were created and unable to afford tuitions to earn degrees in new fields, not to mention the unspoken age discrimination.

—Catherine

As a contract worker in the so-called gig economy, you basically eat what you kill. No work, no pay. And while this may be great for businesses, it's a mixed bag for us plus-fifty workers. At a time when we most need income predictability and security, contract or freelance work offers neither.

I have been taking all kinds of courses to keep my skills current, but you can't get trained on the proprietary software, and no one will teach you. I have been working all kinds of seasonal jobs.

—Kelly

Every year you pass fifty, it gets extremely difficult to find a good-paying job. That's the sad truth. That's another reason to raise the minimum wage—just so that we can survive. You can be healthy and have a proven track record, but many companies just don't care and won't hire you.

—Keith

Making Sense of the New Work Environment

A lot of us are trying to wrap our brains around the new work environment and struggling to make sense of the changes that we see all around us. Some of us are still holding out for good W-2 jobs and are demoralized when job-search strategies that delivered for us in our late thirties and early forties fail us now, in our mid-fifties and early sixties.

Denial shows up in other ways too.

It is refusing to learn and, in the worst case, having a sense of self-righteous disdain for any of the new technologies that make contingency work feasible. Faced with accelerating changes and disruptive technologies, some of us hold tight to old models of work, refusing to budge from what is familiar. Recruiters say that nothing ages us faster.

But wait: Might the shared economy of less structured work offer us a few benefits that we're not considering? True, it's no panacea, and it's definitely not the answer to all of our financial woes. But in this environment, where many of us will have to cobble together multiple income streams to make a living, are we being too quick to dismiss "side gigging" as only for millennials? A growing number of baby boomers are discovering the shared economy and including it as one strategic option in their "work casseroles."

Leveraging Our Assets

The shared economy offers us plus-fifty workers opportunities to supplement our incomes by renting out our assets and not just our homes and cars but also our time, skills, accumulated knowledge, and experiences.

Now, if you're unemployed, independent work, or "gigging," most likely won't replace your old income. Let's not exaggerate what it can deliver. But if funds are tight, it can help with cash flow while you figure out what's next. You may even be able to piece together enough income to put off filing for early social security and avoid reducing your ultimate benefit.

In a lot of cases, independent work allows us to test the waters as "micro-entrepreneurs" without putting capital at risk. And, depending on what we're selling, we can set our own rates, participate part-time, and at least feel like our own bosses.

Also, because nobody really cares how old we are on many of these sharing platforms, gigging offers a path around the rampant age discrimination that so many of us experience when looking for traditional work.

Strapped for cash and facing narrowing work options, more and more older adults are testing the waters as independent workers. Uber, the largest of the ride-sharing services, commissioned a study in 2015 and found that 24.5 percent of its drivers were over fifty.[3]

In fact, Uber has more driver-partners over fifty than under thirty (19 percent) and offers a special incentive to AARP members who sign up.

Airbnb, the world's largest accommodation-sharing site, reports that one in four hosts in the United States are over age fifty, and 13 percent of hosts are over the age of sixty.[4] Seniors constitute the company's fastest-growing segment, in large part due to women, who account for 64 percent of Airbnb's senior hosts.

People are selling anything and everything on these sharing platforms. Below is a small sampling:

Airbnb (https://www.airbnb.com) Offers in-home vacation lodging. Make money by renting out your home, vacation rental, spare bedroom, or couch.

Campspace (https://en.campspace.com) Make money renting out your garden or backyard to campers.

Dogvacay/Catvacay (https://dogvacay.com/lp/catvacay) Love dogs and cats? Make money by providing loving, cage-free care and other services to people's dogs and cats.

Eat With (https://eatwith.com) Make money sharing your passion for food with guests from around the world.

Feastly (https://eatfeastly.com) Love cooking? Make money by creating unique meals for guests in your community.

Fiverr (https://www.fiverr.com) Make money by selling your creative and professional services, ranging from foreign-language translation to voice-overs and logo design.

Freelancer (https://www.freelancer.com) Make money using this freelance marketplace by leveraging your knowledge, experience, and expertise. Start your business completely using this service.

Guru (http://www.guru.com) Make money using this freelance marketplace by leveraging your knowledge, experience, and expertise. Start your business completely with freelancers.

Handy (https://www.handy.com) Earn cash providing professional housecleaning and/or handyman services.

Home Hosted Meals (homehostedmeals.com) Like to cook? Travelers pay for home-hosted meals all over the world. The idea is to meet new people and share meals and cultural insights.

HopSkipDrive (https://www.hopskipdrive.com) Don't want to drive adults around? HopSkipDrive is a ride service for kids designed to help families take the stress out of getting their children home and to their various activities.

Instacart (https://www.instacart.com) Make money by delivering groceries to your neighbors. (Note that you must be able to lift twenty-five pounds to join Instacart.)

Just Park (https://justpark.com) Make money renting out your parking space for a few hours, a weekend, or longer.

Lyft (https://www.lyft.com) Earn extra money by driving your car with Lyft.

Pilotworks (https://pilotworks.com) Love to cook or bake? Earn money starting your own food-based business. Pilotworks operates culinary incubators across the United States and provides specialized products and services to entrepreneurs in the food community to help them bring new companies and ideas to market.

Plate Culture (https://plateculture.com) Join as host and earn money cooking for others.

Postmates (https://postmates.com) Earn cash on your schedule as a courier making deliveries from stores and restaurants.

Rover (https://www.rover.com) Earn money gigging for the nation's largest network of "5-star" pet sitters and dog walkers.

SabbaticalHomes (https://www.sabbaticalhomes.com) Are you an academic? Check out this resource for home exchange, house rental, house sitting, and sharing opportunities.

Schlepit (https://www.schlep.it/#/) Have a truck? Earn cash by helping people move their large or awkward items.

Shared Earth (https://sharedearth.com) Interested in bartering? Shared Earth connects people who have land with people who want to garden or farm.

Skillshare (https://www.skillshare.com) Share your expertise in business, culinary arts, photography, music, writing, and so on. Earn cash by teaching classes in person or online.

Spinlister (https://www.spinlister.com) Make money by renting your bikes, surfboards, or snowboards.

Takelessons (https://takelessons.com) Share your expertise in languages, computers, academic tutoring, music, sports, fitness, and more. You can make money by teaching classes in person or online.

TaskRabbit (https://www.taskrabbit.com) Make money by running errands and doing chores for other people.

Turo (https://turo.com) Car collecting dust? Earn cash by renting it out.

Uber (https://www.uber.com) Make extra money by driving your car with Uber.

Upwork (https://www.upwork.com) Make money on this freelance marketplace by leveraging your knowledge, experience, and expertise. Start your business completely with freelancers.

Varagesale (https://www.varagesale.com) Earn cash by decluttering your home and selling unused items.

Vayable (https://www.vayable.com) Make money by offering tourists an insider's guide to unique local experiences.

Verbling (https://www.verbling.com) Make money teaching others to speak your language.

Wonolo (https://www.wonolo.com) Make money offering your services on this on-demand staffing platform.

Zilok (http://us.zilok.com) Make money by renting out anything, including tools, appliances, musical instruments, and equipment.

99 Designs (https://99designs.com) Make money using your design skills in art, illustrations, logos, Web and app designs, clothing and merchandise designs, and more.

Now, nobody's getting rich by gigging with these companies. Earnings are all over the map, with Airbnb being at the high end. And even then, your take can vary significantly depending on where you're located and whether you're renting a couch or a starter castle.

Drivers for Uber make on average $20 per hour after expenses. But again, depending on where you're driving, you can make significantly less. For example, drivers in Detroit average $6.60 per hour after taxes and expenses; drivers in Houston, $8.43; and drivers in Denver, $11.21.[5]

What people like about the sharing economy is the opportunity to earn supplemental income and the flexibility to work when they want. In the current environment, a lot of us are going to need more than one income stream and more than one hustle to make ends meet. That's what the gig economy offers us: a source of additional cash. It's not a career path, but at our age, a lot of us aren't looking for career paths (or we've stopped looking because we're not getting any traction with our searches).

Health challenges forced me out of my job at fifty-four. My pension was not enough to live on. I didn't know what I was going to do. With Uber, I can drive when I want. The cash comes in handy. Without it, I couldn't live.

—Mandy

Lyft alone is not enough, but when I add what I make driving to my other job I do OK. I will never forget my first fare. I got so turned around with the GPS that I offered to pay the passenger $10 for wasting his time, but he wouldn't take it.

—Walter

Our Shared Economy, or the Sharing-the-Crumbs Economy

Critics have a lot to say about the negatives of independent work defined as contract, contingent, part-time/temporary, and freelance jobs.[6] The concerns are real and are probably well known to you if you've participated in the sharing economy for any length of time.

As a contractor, you generally get no benefits and are responsible for covering your own expenses. There's no health insurance, and you're on your own with social security because your employer is not required to make social security (or Medicare) contributions. And in most cases you're not eligible for unemployment insurance benefits when your contract ends. Forget, too, about labor protections like minimum wage, overtime, and workers' compensation. And because these independent jobs are uncertain and unreliable, there's no income stability.

I'm a graphic designer but have done a little of everything to try to stay afloat: I've been a clothing store cashier and a babysitter. At fifty-nine, I support myself with freelance gigs, but the money is unreliable. I apply for twenty-five or thirty jobs a week but rarely hear back. When I do make it to the interview stage, I'm told that I'm not a good "culture fit." I am up on all the latest technology and social media but look like a middle-aged mom.

To the thirty-somethings, I don't look like I can do cutting-edge design. In December someone hit my car, and I used the $1,500 insurance money to pay my mortgage.

—Quinn

It won't surprise you that the debate rages on about whether the shared economy is good—bringing freedom, choices, and much-needed employment to millions of people—or bad—degrading labor standards, evading regulations, and creating a nation of low-wage, part-time workers. And the debate and its ramifications are not taking place just in the United States.

In Paris, homeowners must be registered with the government and can only rent their homes a maximum of 120 days per year. Last year, authorities cracked down on illegal Airbnb vacation rentals and threatening to remove some 43,000 unregistered homes, 80 percent of Airbnb's Paris rentals, from the space-sharing site.[7]

In Madrid, proposed legislation would limit Airbnb rentals to ninety days per year.[8] In Berlin, authorities, citing the need to protect affordable housing, banned Airbnb rentals to tourists. Restrictions have been eased recently, but steep fines remain for noncompliance with new rules.[9]

Uber, too, continues to face obstacles with local governments and regulators. It recently lost big when Europe's top court classified the ride-hailing service as a transport rather than a technology company and, as such, subjected to the same regulations governing the traditional taxi cab industry.[10] Rulings like this have already forced Uber to restrict or suspend operations in multiple locations, including Finland, France, Germany, Hungary, Spain, and the Netherlands.[11]

Whether we like it or not, the sharing economy is here to stay. Just as we boomers are entering our endgames, all of the work rules are changing. We don't romanticize the sharing economy. We know that we pay a high price for the "freedom and choice" of uncertain work. We should look at gigging with our eyes wide open and as just an option to consider. We must be clear about what it is and what it's not.

But I Don't Want to Drive Uber or Host with Airbnb

You want to return to work, not some part-time gig or contract, but a traditional, nine-to-five old-school job with benefits. You know the odds are against you. You're in your early fifties, maybe even late forties. You've been out of the game for two years or more, maybe much more due to personal or family matters.

You know recruiters don't look favorably on gaps in career history. And no one is banging down your door trying to hire you. Age discrimination is alive and well. But even with all these barriers, you're not ready to throw in the towel, to give up on the hope of returning to work. What you want to know is beyond the usual job-hunting strategies. What else might you consider?

I'm not going to lie to you. If your goal is to work full-time making the same money you made before your "hiatus," the chances of that happening are slim, the longer you've been out of work and the older you are. But one work re-entry resource you may not have considered is the corporate mid-career internship, sometimes called "returnship."

Let me say from the jump, these placements are competitive and not easy to land. Only some tiny percentage of the people who apply get them. That said, I believe in working all the levers at our disposal. What might not work for someone else might work for you.

So, what is a "returnship?" It's a short-term, non-binding, paid work internship for mid-career (and sometimes senior) professionals who voluntarily exited the workforce two or more years ago for any number of reasons and now wish to return. Early re-entry programs focused almost exclusively on hiring women. Corporations were experiencing professional women exiting in droves and not just to take care of their children, but because they were fed up with unsupportive work environments and frustrated by the lack of advancement opportunities.

Corporate returnships were part of a strategy to woo women back. Skilled and experienced women got to return to work after years away. There they could earn income, hone their skills, reconnect with people in their field, and get acclimated to a work environment that had likely changed significantly since they left. Companies could assess fit and performance based on actual assignments and feedback from bosses and colleagues. Women who successfully completed the internship were often offered full-time employment. And even if they weren't hired, the returnship gave them something current and relevant to add to their resume.

Fast forward to today. Many returnships still focus on women, but a growing number of programs also accept male applicants and will consider candidates over fifty.

iRelaunch, founded in 2007, is a pioneer and leader in the job-re-entry space and lists eighty paid corporate re-entry programs around the world. You can find them here: https://www.irelaunch.com/paidcorporateprograms. iRelaunch works directly with nearly forty blue-chip companies to develop, publicize, and identify returning professionals for their career re-entry internship programs. It also hosts two major return to work conferences per year and offers an array of other services including individual coaching, networking events, and classes to update skills.

Below are some other organizations that offer a range of professional services to help facilitate re-entry into the workforce after a long absence.

reacHIRE (http://www.reachire.com) offers proprietary training, customized coaching, and networking opportunities to support women who wish to return to work after a career gap. It helps them find "enternships," full- or part-time positions and develop strategies for redeploying their skills into new areas.

OnRamp Fellowship (http://onrampfellowship.com) is a re-entry platform that matches experienced lawyers returning to the workforce after a career hiatus with law firms and legal departments in the US, Australia, Canada, and UK in year-long paid positions.

Path Forward (http://pathforward.org) is a nonprofit organization that places professionals in the San Francisco Bay Area, Denver, and

New York/New Jersey in mid-career paid internships to help them jump start their careers after time off for caregiving or other family obligations.

I Think I'll Start a Business

Jeri Sedlar, a motivational speaker, a career-transition consultant, and the co-author (with Rick Miners) of *Don't Retire, Rewire!: 5 Steps to Fulfilling Work That Fuels Your Passion, Suits Your Personality and Fills Your Pocket*, describes the two kinds of people who start businesses as follows: "those who always planned to and those who cannot find a job." I chuckled in recognition when I read that. It's so true.

You're going to read a lot about the rising rate of so-called encore entrepreneurs over the age of fifty. Often these are cheery little articles picturing beaming boomers standing in front of their recently launched pizza parlors, florist shops, or dry-cleaning businesses.

You're going to hear about Julia Child, Edith Pearlman, Colonel Sanders, and others who started businesses well into their forties, fifties, and sixties, and look what they achieved—and so can you!

You're going to be told to keep your chin up when your business flounders or fails; that lots of businesses find success only after multiple failures; and that you should just keep at it.

In your gut, you know that something is wrong with this picture. You're slaving away as a solo entrepreneur: chief cook and bottle washer. At least when you were working, you had some support. But now you're doing *everything*: clerical work, bookkeeping, sales, follow-ups, R & D, and more. You have ten jobs instead of one.

And it's not like you're making the big bucks. Now, you may be OK with that if the main reason for starting your venture was to bring fulfillment and purpose to your life. But if entrepreneurship was your plan B, a last resort when you ran out of money, couldn't find a job, and started running on fumes, pursuing your passion may seem like a bit of a luxury. Making money to stay afloat is your primary concern.

I'm a self-employed contractor. I guess I'm independent. Now I work for three crazy bosses instead of one.

—Tony

With the median household net worth for boomers lower today than it was in the mid-eighties, you'd think entrepreneurship, with all of its attendant financial risks, would be off the table. After all, it takes money to make money. Yet, over the last two decades, a growing number of boomers have taken the leap.

I was laid off at fifty-one. Didn't even bother trying to find a job or getting unemployment. Just built up my own company. I had worked for myself before, and in my industry it's not unusual for people to work for themselves. It took about one and a half years for me to get myself back up to essentially full-time employment, but I'm there now and about to celebrate four years in business.

—Sheri

According to the Ewing Marion Kauffman Foundation, a leader in advancing entrepreneurship, about one-quarter (25.5 percent) of all new entrepreneurs are over fifty-five, compared to only 14.8 percent in 1996.[12] Based on the media's accounts of these boomers, you'd think all of these older entrepreneurs were small-business owners and managers hanging out their shingles on Main Street. But in empirical studies, self-employment is used as a numerical proxy for entrepreneurship, and the rate of self-employment increases as we get older. So it's likely that the boom in boomer entrepreneurs is a result of the rising numbers of self-employed people working from home.

And there's no problem with that. In fact, 92 percent of all businesses in the United States are microenterprises comprising between one and five employees, including the owner.[13] Eighty-two percent of American firms have no paid employees at all.

144

The high proportion of self-employed older entrepreneurs may also explain why businesses started by boomers tend to have lower economic impacts overall. According to the Ewing Marion Kauffman Foundation 2015 State of Entrepreneurship Address, "entrepreneurial activity among aging boomers could also turn out to be less economically significant. Self-employment rates rise with age, and older groups are more likely to be self-employed than their younger counterparts are, but self-employment adds less to growth than entrepreneurship does."

We also want to distinguish so-called growth entrepreneurs from lifestyle entrepreneurs. When Gallup surveyed 2,000 boomer-aged entrepreneurs and non-entrepreneurs, 59 percent said that a lifestyle choice (achieving independence and following their passions) had been their main reason for starting their businesses.[14] Only 10 percent said they had "an idea for a product/service that [met] an unfulfilled need in the marketplace," which business experts say is a prerequisite for starting a successful venture.

In the start-up ecosystem, where growth is king, it's rare to find a business that was formed just to provide a great quality of life and some income for its owner. But maybe we boomers have learned a little something about work-life balance. In our fifties and sixties, most of us are not looking for eighty-hour workweeks, home-run swings, and $100 million exits. That doesn't mean that we don't want to be engaged or work hard and with purpose. But for many of us, the idea of some venture totally taking over our lives is just not that appealing.

And because a lot of boomers who start businesses are some combination of lifestyle and "necessity" entrepreneurs, funds to invest in these new enterprises are very limited if they exist at all. All of this has programmatic implications for organizations focused on helping older entrepreneurs establish and nurture their businesses.

Realistic input on what constitutes a viable business idea, financing options (especially bank loans under $250,000), and technologies that help entrepreneurs work smarter, not harder, are key. And given the dominance of the grow, grow, grow start-up ecosystem, it's going to take some sharp elbows to create room (and support) for lifestyle businesses, many of which are small by design.

I'm Not Done Yet

But what if you want more than a lifestyle business to pay the bills and keep boredom at bay? You want another big bite at the apple, another shot at making it big. You don't talk about it much because . . . well, who starts a business in their fifties? Pure foolishness, right?! At a certain age, surely, we're too old to be thinking about anything entrepreneurial, especially something big and demanding.

You might be surprised to learn that a new study by MIT and the Kellogg School of Business busts the ageist myth that older adults just can't cut it as entrepreneurs.[15] The MIT/Kellogg study looked at 2.7 million business owners who launched companies between 2007 and 2014 and the data showed that a fifty-year-old is nearly twice as likely to start a top or very successful business as someone two decades younger.

The study also found that the "average age of start up founders is 42 and the average age of entrepreneurs who founded high growth companies is 45."[16] This, of course, flies in the face of conventional wisdom, which would have us believe that the typical hot-shot start-up entrepreneur is a twenty-year-old working out of his parents' garage. In fact, according to the research, "20-something founders have the lowest likelihood of starting a company with a successful exit."

So, if you do have a big entrepreneurial idea you'd like to pursue, don't rule yourself out based on age alone. If you have the experience, skills, stamina, and confidence, at least take the next step to see if your business idea is viable. And if you need to beef up your business leadership skills, the internet has lots of sites that offer excellent self-paced educational resources. Here's a link to a list of ten great websites that offer business courses for free. Yes, for *free*.

https://www.inc.com/larry-kim/10-incredible-websites-that-teach
-business-leadership-skills-for-free.html

Obviously, one big study is not going wipe out the rampant ageism that exists in the marketplace and the entrepreneurship ecosystem. But let us not buy into the youth myth by drinking the Kool-Aid
ourselves.

Cultivating an Entrepreneurial Mind-set

Let's face it, many of us just don't see ourselves launching a business,
big or small—viewing it as just too risky, given our particular circumstances. But even if it is not our thing, we can still benefit from
cultivating an entrepreneurial mind-set.

In the new normal of financial vulnerability, we don't get to do
what we've always done. Having an entrepreneurial mind-set means
being open to changes, open to new ways of doing things, and open
to doing things we've never done before.

It means learning to live with ambiguity and uncertainty.

It means experimenting, doing small tests, learning from mistakes, and adapting.

It means moving outside of our familiar comfort zone and inviting in diverse others as mentors, allies, partners, collaborators, and
coconspirators.

It means deciding which risks are acceptable and taking that next
step.

It means being curious and embracing lifelong learning and technology.

It means being resilient, assessing our losses, and doing what we
need to do to recover quickly.

And it means speaking up and advocating for our interests and
ourselves.

This book grew out of an entrepreneurial mind-set. I believe that
the most powerful ideas often come from our efforts to solve our

own problems. Unprepared for retirement, I could not find what I needed in the books I was reading. After talking to friends in the same boat, I realized that I was not alone.

I asked myself what I could do from where I was sitting. What skills, resources, and relationships did I have that I could bring to bear?

I knew I could write, speak, do research, and find kindred spirits online.

My first blog post with *Next Avenue* was well received, which let me know that what was happening to my friends and me was widespread. As I wrote more, I started hearing from people and forming relationships with them. Ideas turned into collaborations that culminated in *55, Underemployed, and Faking Normal* and the Resilience Circles.

Small acts of entrepreneurship can take other forms as well, creating springboards for us to test new waters. It's when we move to a new city, or downsize from the family home, or start that blog, or take that photography class. It's when we exit a toxic relationship or say yes to a new love. It's when we empty our closet of all of those clothes that don't fit or finally get rid of that junk in our basement. It's when we finally take that first step to turn a passion into a livelihood.

Leveraging Your Network

If you're among the long-term unemployed and in your fifties or older, you'll start to notice that your professional network is not what it used to be. Many of your contacts have retired or been sidelined or pushed out. A few have even died. You're out of the loop and no longer getting calls about jobs that haven't been posted yet. In fact, you're not on anybody's short list.

At around age fifty or so you realize that your effort to build a great career is useless, because your time in the center of the action is done. Past life. You apply for jobs, but as you attempt to fill out applications, you realize that your job history has disappeared like bread crumbs on the trail. People move on, retire, and die. Nobody knows you or what you did anymore.

—Ben

You've told me that your friends who are still in jobs with real clout and hiring authority just aren't that helpful. It's not like you're asking them to put forward someone who's unqualified. You have the skills and experience. You just need them to make the introduction—to get you in the room with the decision maker. You can take it from there.

At this stage, it does not work to apply online to some recruitment drop box. Your age is going to screen you out. You have to be green-lighted by someone on the inside. You have to be "on-ramped." I used to get frustrated that fifty- and sixty-something cohorts didn't do more to help. Then I realized a lot of them are barely hanging on themselves and are just trying to coast to retirement without rocking the boat.

—Pamela

My last four gig assignments came from mid-level managers in their thirties and forties. I've noticed that many of us don't include those kinds of people in our professional and social networks. But often they're the people who know what jobs are coming down the pike before they're advertised, and who have the inside scoop on the funding priorities, and who know where the money is.

But I don't have strong ties with the Gen Xers who've helped me, and I wouldn't consider them to be part of my tight inner circle.

In their book, *Repurpose Your Career: A Practical Guide for Baby Boomers*, Marc Miller and Susan Lahey make the case that a casual acquaintance, or a "weak tie"—like a friend of a friend, some guy in a related field whom you met at a conference, or a former office mate you see only occasionally—might be a better resource for jobs and information than a close friend, or a "strong tie." Our close friends and family may actually know too much about our struggles and challenges. But we don't tend to share our struggles with our more distant connections, which makes those relationships less complicated and easier to navigate. With casual acquaintances, we're freer to ask directly for what we want.

In his groundbreaking article, "The Strength of Weak Ties," Mark Granovetter adds that our weak ties are more likely to bring us into contact with networks outside of our circles, exposing us to work opportunities and information about jobs, deals, start-ups, and more that our friends don't know about.[17]

It is easier than ever to exist in information silos and to interact only with people who are just like us. On the work-search front, this puts us at a distinct disadvantage.

No one is saying that cultivating our weak ties or networking with Gen Xers alone is the answer to our economic woes. There is no one answer. Instead, we have a menu of strategic choices from which to pick, based on what makes sense for us, given our particular situation.

We need affirmative action to hire seniors. There is mass discrimination in society, and employers just don't hire us. Someone needs to start legislation and to make sure employers hire a certain percentage of senior citizens. Most people want to work from the ages of fifty-five to seventy-five, and they should be able to do so without prejudice.

—Sandra

Get Off Your Throne

I just took an eight-hour round-trip bus ride to a meeting I thought important that I attend. During my years in corporate America, I did a lot of first- and business-class air travel. Twice I even flew Concorde. But yesterday I put my buns on that bus for a tiny fraction of what it would have cost to fly or take the train. I made a meeting I needed to make. I got off my throne.

What getting off my throne also means is taking a number of small jobs I would have rejected before jobs, I could do in my sleep, minor editing gigs and one-on-one tutoring just to smooth my cash flow. When money is tight for Zoe, the communications professional profiled earlier, she writes press releases for small-dollar clients. "That's my version of taking the bus," she said. "I hate doing press releases at this stage of my career. That's work I'd normally assign to an assistant."

We do what we have to do. That is not the same as saying that we're destined to do work that we hate or that we should stop seeking work aligned with our talents, values, and interests. But it is saying that in the new normal, we're going to have to let go of this notion that our values and worth are based solely on our titles, incomes, and jobs.

We're going to have to let go of our vanity and pride too. We may not get the incomes that we're used to. We may not get the titles and the other perks.

Think in terms of making a casserole of interesting work with two or three income streams.

I just got a part-time board-liaison job that pays half of what I am used to making. I see it as a base to build on. I work three days a week, including one day from home. I am looking for two additional assignments to fill out the week. The board job covers my basic expenses. Anything else would be extra.

—Patricia

Reinvention

The media likes midlife-reinvention stories—the more dramatic, the better. We hear about the fifty-seven-year-old accountant who's making a new career as an opera singer or the lawyer turned pastry chef.

Too often these cheery little tales about following your passion gloss over the practical challenges and pitfalls.

> *After thirty years working overseas with bilateral and multilateral development-aid agencies, my dream was to work here at home helping disenfranchised youth get connected to the workforce. I researched organizations, wrote the compelling letter, reached out to dozens of people, and heard from a tiny handful. I just got no traction. After eighteen months of "We don't want you," my dream of integrating my previous experience into a new profession was replaced by a need for cash flow.*
>
> —Derek

We wonder how these reinvented people are paying their bills. Even if we knew who we wanted to become, how would we manage it? How would we get the training and coaching we needed to ease our midlife transitions to purpose and a paycheck? From where we're standing, sharp turns and sudden moves don't seem like good ideas. *Exhausting* is the word that comes to mind. And when finances are shaky, going for broke on some brand-new endeavor seems just plain risky, not brave.

That doesn't mean that we don't want fulfilling work and meaningful lives. Sure, a few of our contemporaries are taking their retirement desserts and heading off on perpetual vacations. But a lot of us can't or don't want to stop working and are totally up for new career ambitions and totally up for leveraging our skills, experiences, and abilities to tackle new sets of problems.

But we face one barrier after another. Age discrimination is staring us in the face. It's not unusual to hear of folks at the top of their game who send out hundreds if not thousands of résumés and can count on one hand the number of responses they receive.[18]

> *In this country, we live in a youthful world, and women over a certain age are invisible. Unfortunately, we discuss injustice*

and debate what to do about it, but the problem has existed for many years and will continue to exist. Women in their fifties are in a void majority and must be creative in finding new ways of living. The time of being silent is over. Being in need is not a failure. Staying quiet is a failure.

—Collette

When I visit with my friends in New York City it seems odd to see women my age with bright reddish hair. I asked one friend how come she is still coloring her hair. She is almost eighty. She said she had a lot of younger friends and wanted to fit in. But to me she just looked like an eighty-year-old with orange hair.

—Toni

And one of the ironies is that a lot of hiring managers in our age group aren't yet acting as advocates for us. Some even pull up the drawbridge when they see us coming. It's just ridiculous.

I think it is little wonder why we are where we are today as a country. A lot of our talent is sitting on the sidelines, waiting to be put back in the game. Let's make our own pickup game.

—Bruce

I met my recruiter and his boss in the lobby before my interview. It was funny being ushered in by two twenty-somethings that could have been my sons. The interviewer called my name and looked right through me, assuming one of the young recruiters was the candidate. When I approached her she looked at me with what appeared to be disbelief and amusement. We had what I thought was a good interview, with her speaking to me more like a peer than someone vying to be her subordinate (maybe that wasn't a good sign). It was clear I could handle the work. Eventually I got the call from the recruiter. It was a tough call, he said, but they went with someone with more experience.

It was great to be considered, but at fifty-one I know the job market phase is over for me. Turns out I shaved my beard for nothing.

—Robert

Missing Workers

Traditional work options are not cutting it for a lot of people, especially those over fifty-five. This might explain the large number of so-called missing workers. These are would-be job seekers who, because of tenuous job opportunities, have just given up looking for work altogether.

And the number in this category is big and growing.

According to a 2016 Harris Poll of unemployed Americans over the age of eighteen, 43 percent have stopped looking for a job, and nearly 60 percent of those out of work for two years or more have completely given up looking for work. In fact, more than half of the respondents reported that they hadn't been on a job interview since 2014.[19]

If you've been looking for a job and haven't found one, these stats probably won't surprise you. The Harris Poll just validates your instincts. Nearly 30 percent of the respondents were over fifty, and that age group has the second-largest number of unemployed workers.

How many rejection letters (if you hear back at all) do you need to figure out that the traditional world of work is just not that receptive to people our age? We can keep going where we're not wanted, or we can begin to find another way. We know that pioneering new directions is not easy. But what choice do we have?

We're in the midst of a seismic shift—a great transformation. The old and the new are vying for the same space. The ground underneath us is moving whether we move with it or not. Ours is the first generation to experience the so-called longevity bonus—that is, an additional twenty-five to thirty years of life.

Tens of millions of us boomers are making the trek into this new territory, and behind us are tens of millions more. Going first is always the hardest. Those who go first go before there are rules, established pathways, supportive laws, policies, networks, and role models. First is making a path by walking.

Bridging the Gap

Radical reinvention is not for most people. But lots of us want to build on our past careers and use our knowledge, skills, and abilities to serve new purposes in late middle age and beyond.

And as senior knowledge professionals, we have a lot to offer: we have experience, histories, interests, skills, insights, and hobbies, and we've learned from our failures, near misses, and successes big and small. We need help figuring out what is applicable to new industries and what can be cross-woven into new ventures. What work can we boomers do with one another, and what can we do with allies who "get" this moment of transformation?

There's a lot of chaos out there. What happened before is a poor guide for what will happen in the future. We need path-finding solutions. We're going to have to make our own way.

—Art

It's not easy being part of the advance team that's ushering in a new era of aging options. It seems that everywhere we look, there is rampant age discrimination, stereotyping, and what Lorraine Banfield, author of *Second Act Soul Calls: Your Guide for the Re-Invention of Your Life at Midlife and Beyond with Passion, Purpose and Possibilities*, calls "first act ideas."

This is why we're going to need "bridge work" to pay the bills while we figure out how and where to land. And that bridge work could be cool or could look crazy at times, depending on how you're used to rolling. You could be an adjunct professor at a local university, a sales associate at the Container Store, a dog walker, a Lyft driver, or you could find a cool consulting gig in Mexico.

We're going to need tribes of like-minded individuals who engage with us, push us, and share their stories with us but also stick with us when the times get rough. And rough times come with this territory. That's why you need your Resilience Circle: it offers you a community, a docking station, and a place to speak candidly and to share information, ideas, and resources. It's a place where you can exhale.

And while it may feel like we're alone, there are a growing number of organizations, programs, initiatives, allies, and advocates that support a new work imperative for aging Americans.

And let's face it: we don't all want the same things.

Some of us want to get back into the nine-to-five job market, and some of us want to get out of it altogether. Some of us are trying, with mixed success, to cobble together a casserole of different work assignments (the kinds that require 1099 tax forms). Others are testing the gig economy as micro-entrepreneurs. Others have dreams of becoming "encore" entrepreneurs and launching their own businesses. And a lot of us are doing mind-numbing bridge work to stay afloat until we figure out what's next.

The list below is by no means exhaustive, but it's intended to give you a flavor of the kind of organizations out there to help. These organizations, and others like them, are like our Sherpas. They can help us navigate the trek across this new territory. You may not agree with all of their philosophies and offerings. Just pick what makes sense for your situation. Keep in mind, too, that we're still in the early days of inhabiting this new land, and no one has it all figured out. Most of us are just making it up as we go along.

AARP (https://www.aarp.org) is the nation's largest nonprofit organization dedicated to empowering Americans fifty and older to choose how they live as they age.

AARP Foundation's BACK TO WORK 50+ Program (https://www.aarp.org/aarp-foundation/our-work/income/back-to-work-50-plus/) is AARP's charitable affiliate helping vulnerable older adults to build economic opportunity and social connectedness. BACK TO WORK 50+ provides services and resources to help older, low-income workers access jobs that are in high demand.

The Age of No Retirement (https://www.ageofnoretirement.org) aims to shatter age-related barriers and ageist stereotypes to create an age-inclusive future.

BoomerWorks (http://www.boomerworks.org) offers coaching and workshops to older adults to help them find work in the new gig economy.

The Conscious Elder Network (http://www.consciouselders.org/) is an educational nonprofit organization of elders dedicated to working intergenerationally for social and economic justice, environmental stewardship, and sound governance.

The Diana Davis Spencer Foundation Fellowship (http://www.global goodfund.org/apply) works under the auspices of the Global Good Fund. This fellowship is for entrepreneurs of all ages who are creating and cultivating US-based job opportunities for individuals over fifty years of age.

Education Pioneers (http://www.educationpioneers.org/who-we-are) recruits and develops talented students and experienced professionals from diverse backgrounds to work for K–12 school districts, charter schools, and other education organizations. It operates in Austin, Chicago, Connecticut, Dallas–Fort Worth, the DC metro area, Denver, Greater Boston, Greater Los Angeles, Houston, Kansas City, Memphis, Nashville, Newark, New Jersey, New Orleans, New York City, the San Francisco Bay Area and Tulsa.

Encore (http://encore.org/fellowships/) matches skilled, seasoned professionals with social purpose organizations in high-impact, paid transitional assignments.

Experience Matters (http://experiencemattersaz.org/) connects the skills and talents of experienced adults in the Phoenix area with the diverse needs of nonprofit organizations.

Fifty+ (http://fiftyplus.ywcasf-marin.org) is a program at the YWCA San Francisco and Marin that helps women achieve economic security through employment. The program provides a targeted mix of services and strategies to improve its clients' job readiness.

The Global Institute for Experienced Entrepreneurship (http://expe rieneurship.com/about-giee.php) is changing the negative paradigm of aging by building an "Experienced Economy" and by helping governments and corporations around the world see the potential of the largest talent pool of experience in human history.

HelpAge USA (http://www.helpage.org) helps older people claim their rights, challenge discrimination, and overcome poverty so that they can lead dignified, secure, active, and healthy lives.

The Institute for Career Transitions (http://www.ictransitions.org) is an educational not-for-profit, founded by MIT-based scholars, whose mission is to research, validate, and teach the new realities of maintaining one's well-being while navigating career disruptions. ICT seeks to improve economic outcomes and well-being for older professionals navigating career transitions through personalized support in an innovative work-in-between-work environment by applying research-based strategies for generating sustainable livelihoods.

The International Association of Jewish Vocational Services (http://www.iajvs.org) is a not-for-profit association linking twenty-nine health and human service agencies in the United States, Canada, and Israel that provide a wide range of educational and vocational-rehabilitation services. Through its member agencies, individuals seeking to improve their lives gain access to a wide array of services, such as career management advice, skills training, rehabilitation, and mental health and health services.

International Longevity Center Global Alliance (http://www.ilc

-alliance.org/index.php/home) (ILC Global Alliance) is a multinational consortium of organizations. It helps societies address longevity and population aging in positive and productive ways, typically using a life-course approach and highlighting older people's productivity and contributions to family and society as a whole. The ILC Alliance includes centers in the United States and sixteen other countries.

Iona (https://www.iona.org) has been serving the Washington metropolitan area for over forty years, offering support, consultation, and advice on how to navigate the challenges of caring for or supporting an older adult and answering our questions about our own aging journey.

The Ewing Marion Kauffman Foundation (https://www.kauffman.org) helps to empower makers, doers, and dreamers to create their own destinies and achieve uncommon things. It is an excellent online resource helping entrepreneurs to start and grow their businesses.

LeadingAge (http://www.leadingage.org) is a trusted voice for aging focused on education, advocacy, and applied research. It has some 6,000-plus members and partners including not-for-profit organizations representing the entire field of aging services, including thirty-eight state partners, hundreds of business, consumer groups, foundations, and research partners.

The National Caucus and Center on Black Aging (http://www.ncba-aged.org) advocates for African Americans and minority seniors in the areas of employment, health and wellness, and affordable housing.

The National Council on Aging (https://www.ncoa.org) improves the health and economic security of older adults through provision of a variety of practical tools, services, and programs including the BenefitsCheck-up, My Medicare Matters, and the Aging Mastery Program.

The National Older Workers Career Center (https://www.nowcc.org) promotes an age-diverse workforce through the expansion of part-time and full-time employment opportunities in government agencies for skilled and experienced individuals fifty-five and over.

The New Start Career Network (https://www.newstartcareernet work.org) provides older (age 45 and older) long-term unemployed job seekers in New Jersey with access to free, personalized career services, including Web-based information resources and in-person and virtual career coaching.

Peace Corps Response (https://www.peacecorps.gov/volunteer/is -peace-corps-right-for-me/peace-corps-response) sends experienced professionals to undertake short-term, high-impact service assignments in communities around the world. The Peace Corps does not have an age limit, and you can serve with your spouse or partner. Also see volunteering at age fifty-plus (https://www.peacecorps.gov /volunteer/is-peace-corps-right-for-me/50plus).

Platform to Employment (http://www.platformtoemployment.com/) addresses the need for the long-term unemployed to return to work. The program combines job-readiness training, personal and family support services, financial counseling, and a paid work experience. It operates in Cincinnati, Chicago, Dallas, Denver, Detroit, Indianapolis, Las Vegas, Minneapolis, Newark, San Diego, San Francisco, and Tampa. Other municipal and state governments are considering replicating the model.

Prosperity Now, formerly the Corporation for Enterprise Development (https://prosperitynow.org), works at the local, state, and federal levels to expand prosperity for all US families. It offers a unique combination of scalable practical solutions, in-depth research, and proven policy solutions, all aimed at building wealth for those who need it most.

The Radical Age Movement (RAM) (https://radicalagemovement .org) is a national nonprofit based in New York City dedicated to confronting ageism is all its forms through education, raising consciousness, social action, and the creation of a national network of RAM chapters.

The Renaissance Entrepreneurship Center (http://www.rencenter.org) is located in the Bay Area and helps underserved individuals from socially and economically diverse backgrounds (including women, people of color, and older entrepreneurs) start businesses.

ReServe (http://www.reserveinc.org) matches continuing professionals over the age of fifty-five with organizations that need their expertise. It operates in Baltimore, South Florida, Milwaukee, Newark, New York City, and Westchester County.

The Second Shift (https://www.thesecondshift.com) gives professional women a clear path to remain in the workforce when full-time employment is not an option.

Self-Employment Assistance (http://workforcesecurity.doleta.gov/un employ/self.asp) is a federally sponsored program under the Department of Labor that allows states to offer entrepreneurship training to dislocated and unemployed workers interested in starting their own businesses. To date, only Delaware, Mississippi, New Hampshire, New York, and Oregon have active SEA programs.

Senior Planet (https://seniorplanet.org) is the first tech-themed resource for people sixty and up who are living and aging with attitude.

Senior Service America (http://www.seniorserviceamerica.org) is one of America's oldest and largest operators of employment programs for America's seniors. SSA manages the Department of Labor–funded Senior Community Service Employment Program (SCSEP) in thirteen states, providing income, training, and work experience to older adults in financial jeopardy.

SHIFT (http://shiftonline.org) is a Twin Cities–based community organization for people who are navigating midlife work-life transitions. It helps members create pathways to meaningful and sustainable lives.

SilverBills (https://www.silverbills.com) receives and scrutinizes subscribers' bills and ensures that they are paid correctly and on time. The advocacy and monitoring function goes beyond traditional bill pay services offered by banks.

The Transition Network (http://www.thetransitionnetwork.org/about-ttn) is a national organization and inclusive community of professional women over fifty whose changing life situations lead them to seek new connections, resources, and opportunities. Through small-group interactions, programs, and workshops, members inspire and support each other to continue a life of learning, engagement, and leadership in the world.

Troops to Teachers (http://www.proudtoserveagain.com) is a Department of Defense program designed to assist eligible military personnel who want to teach in public schools as their second careers.

The US Small Business Administration and AARP Summer Encore Mentoring (https://www.sba.gov/encorementoring) have a strategic partnership and jointly counsel, train, and mentor encore entrepreneurs on the creation of small businesses.

Workaway (https://www.workaway.info) is a global cultural exchange program where a person offers a few hours of volunteering in exchange for food and accommodation. Hosts prefer more experienced workers who have specific skills.

Workforce50.com (http://www.workforce50.com) is a career site for boomers, seniors, and experienced workers. Its core mission is to find and provide job listings from employers interested in hiring people fifty and older.

Meet Brandon

This is Brandon's story in his own words:
I thought I was working in the job I'd retire from years later. That is what I hoped for. I'd just attended a companywide meeting where a couple of people had been feted for their twenty years of service. I got a tear in my eye thinking about how wonderful that must have been—how secure those folks must have felt.

But my former company didn't care about my hopes or dreams. The next week I was laid off, along with forty other colleagues. So I was out of a job and fifty-six. Nothing was happening. But one good thing had happened—something that I think was cosmic. I'd purchased two suits and a laptop just days before being laid off. That was the universe looking out for me and preparing me for the new path ahead.

I began applying for positions similar to my work as an account manager. One of my former clients even hired me to do day-to-day operations in his office for about one-third of my previous salary. I knew going in that it would be a temporary job and wasn't surprised when it ended eighteen months later.

I have a family. My wife and grade school–aged children were doing all right before the layoff. Now my wife has found work in her longtime profession as a photographer, but our income is under strain. We've cut back on our expenses, but we've always been debt averse, so we don't have a lot of bills. We've also been able to get a great deal of help from my wife's mother. It is certain that without her help—she provided a loan and bought some of the kids' clothing for school—we'd be much worse off. If you can get help from your extended family, do not refuse it. One reason I need to work is to keep my family from worrying about anything.

Plus I want my children to see me going to work and providing for them. I'm provincial in that way.

So I continued applying for the same account manager and customer service work that I knew, but it just wasn't working. I kept seeing the same language in carefully worded rejection emails: "We found other candidates for the position who would be a better fit." *Better fit*, as if I were a shoe that was too large, or the organization was too large for my skills. No, I presumed that my rejections had to do with other factors.

I was too experienced or too old for the millennials they were then in the habit of hiring. I might not be adaptable or malleable enough for them. I might not work well with all of those younger people. Granted, even at sixty, I don't see myself as old. I'm still trying to grasp the weight of longevity's impact on my existence in a working world where most of the employees are in their thirties and forties.

I admit that there was another problem with my job search. I wasn't looking for work that I thought was *beneath* my experience and education. In a time when almost any legal income would've helped, I had no business not pursuing any kind of work. Many people work in places far below their stations to support their families. I needed to get down from that high horse.

To keep my head up during this time out of work, I networked and stayed active. I intensified my artistic work. That meant continuing to write my poetry and short stories and to make greater progress on a play I'd been writing. I also began using my phone's camera in earnest. My wife suggested that I create a blog. I hemmed and hawed about the idea for a few months. In the end, I decided to create a Tumblr site where I could post anything I wanted to without having to crash through learning-curve guardrails by using something more complicated.

I started by uploading poems, a few cuts of the music that

I'd posted on my SoundCloud, and my photographs. Eventually, the only things I uploaded were photographs. I traversed the city, capturing the murals of other artists in detail. I'd supply information about the muralists, even supplying links to their sites or other work. I considered myself providing a service, since I also linked to my Tumblr site, Sonny Jam's Place, and my Facebook page.

People liked the work, I enjoyed the "discoveries," and I stayed active. Eventually, I began to work on my own photographic images. I saw something worthy of being captured everywhere. I love clouds and reflections, so my street photography became my focus. I took so many photographs that I realized that I had a collection. I saw the potential for an exhibit. I still do. An artist friend loaned me his large-format ink-jet printer. It allowed me to see whether these smartphone-camera shots looked good when printed at sizes larger than four inches. They did.

After my eighteen-month stint in my former client's office, I spent a great deal of time in my local library. A librarian saw me reading a book on writing and invited me to a writers' workshop. Now I'm participating in it with several writers, and we critique and revise our work. It keeps us active.

After several more application rejections and even interviews, I began to think of the cliché that goes something like this: "Crazy is doing the same thing over and over and expecting different results." Maybe I wasn't going to find work as an account manager ever again. Perhaps that career path was covered in weeds and bear traps. I adjusted my résumé, shortened it, and made changes to interest certain employers. I changed my cover letter's style, and I began pursuing different leads.

Another cosmic thing happened. I got a call from a woman who said she kept seeing my name on LinkedIn. In this connected world of social networks, the only thing we shared was our one mutual friend. That friend told me later that this woman—I'll call her Sandy—did that often. Sandy's profession was life coaching, but she never asked me for money. Sandy advised me that I needed to figure out how my skills were transferable and how I might turn my experience down another path. My time as an account manager with a long-term job and a salary was over. The conversation lasted ninety minutes. I accepted her advice. Sandy didn't help me find a job, but she helped me shift my energy and reset my headspace. One thing is certain: I will not be "out here" for as long as before. My energy is different.

Here are my suggestions:

- Stay active. The depression that some of us may unknowingly develop can be paralyzing. Make certain that you have things to do outside of your home that cost little or nothing. Libraries and museums work.

- Intensify or reinvigorate your sidelined artistic endeavors. We always lament the lack of time to write, read, or paint. Now is the time to get going. Embrace your multitalented self. Do more than one thing, and then gravitate toward what feels better.

- Keep a journal. In fact, keep several, each with a different purpose. I have a daily journal that I use to get thoughts out of my head. It's my *diary*, if you will. I keep that in my back pocket. I keep a blank notebook for drawing and for those "morning pages" that unclutter the mind (and I don't read them afterward). I also keep an everyday journal just to keep track of what I do/did during the day (e.g., "applied for this, spoke to so-and-so, went to the grocery store, and wrote"). Without it, my days would blend into one another. You don't want to lose track of your days.

- Never accept anyone who thinks that you're old. Keep in mind that when most of us were born, forty was middle age, and when someone hit sixty, he or she was put out to pasture. We now have people just hitting their strides or figuring out *that something* at sixty-five. Embrace the changes. Force the changes that you'll need to move forward. The only things that you should consider *old* are the ways you used to be.

Menial or Meaningful

Remember to do the "Top This" exercise and to have three minutes of silence.

As I have said, if you make it to sixty-five years old in good health, there's a good chance that you'll live for another couple of decades, that's a long runway if cash is an issue for you. That's why figuring out this income piece is so critical.

◆ How bad is your situation on a scale of one to five?

- Your situation is a "one" if you're caught up on most things or at least not so far behind that anything is about to be repossessed or turned off. Savings? What savings?

- Your situation is a "two" if you're behind on payments for at least one major obligation—like your residence or your vehicle—and several smaller ones, but your creditors are working with you. Small contracts allow you to pay minimum balances if you rob Peter to pay Paul.

- A "three" is the same as a "two," except your creditors are *not* working with you because you haven't contacted them, because they're playing hardball, or for some other reason.

- Your situation is a "four" if you're in danger of losing your house, being evicted from your apartment, or having your mobile phone and utilities cut off. Your contract or income is erratic or nonexistent. Even paying minimum balances is a stretch.

- "Five" is the same as "four," except the IRS is involved.

◆ Remember, this is a no-judgment zone. Finally saying where you are and knowing that others have walked in your shoes will help. If you're a "two" now but have been a "five," talk about what you did to claw your way back. If you're a "one" now but used to be a "three," talk about how you recovered, what worked, and what didn't work. Don't get stuck in a story with a lot of extraneous details. Try to stay at the treetops, not in the weeds. But do share the beautiful and the unbeautiful, the wrong paths you took, your insights and realizations, and the hard lessons you learned.

- How much do you need to live meaningfully? Each person will define *meaningfully* differently. Let's just focus on the number. What's that monthly dollar figure for you? When you look at that number, does it strike you as pure fantasy, or can you envision a pathway to attaining it?

- What's the difference between that number and what you're earning now? When you're sixty-nine, will you still be able to hit that number?

- If you're in the pure fantasy camp, what's taking the number over the top? Is it your housing costs, the city you're living in, or your neighborhood, or something else? What are you willing to do to get that number down?

- Are you depending on one income source? Have you exhausted all avenues for generating additional income sources? What are you willing to do to get this number up?

- Are you being realistic about your prospects in the traditional nine-to-five job market? What validates your optimism? If traditional work turns out not to be an option, what's your plan B?

- Are Gen Xers part of your professional network? Do you have loose ties that you are not tapping, not utilizing? How might you begin to leverage this resource, to cultivate it?

- What bridge work are you having to do to make ends meet? Can you look at bridge work as just strategy, as what we have to do in the meantime until we figure out better next steps? Sometimes even jobs we don't want offer opportunities for learning and growth. Deloris, fifty-one and a lawyer, worked as a sales associate in the gift department at Neiman Marcus during the holidays. "I was embarrassed to be there but made the best of it. I liked learning about fine china, silver, and crystal stemware. I don't plan to be stuck here forever. One day this knowledge will come in handy." Are there any unexpected benefits from the bridge work you're doing? Could there be if you shifted how you think about this work?

◆ Do you have an entrepreneurial mind-set? Leonard A. Schlesinger and Charles F. Kiefer, in their book *Just Start: Take Action, Embrace Uncertainty, Create the Future*, talk about acting quickly with the means at hand, assessing your acceptable loss, bringing other people along, and building on what you find/learn. Do you have an idea you've been noodling around? How might you apply these principles to that idea?

Chapter 10

Thinking Outside
the ~~Box~~ Country

*I am making my peace with never having a job again, which
I think is realistic . . . It's been a life of great effort, huge obstacles, endless work hours, and commuting, and then . . . zip.
Kind of the inverse of the American dream, which is why people
won't even face the reality of what happened to people like me.
It is so unbelievable to them, they would rather cut us out than
face that this could happen to them.*

—Sue

For a lot of us, social security is our retirement plan. The average
monthly benefit in 2018 is $1,404, or $16,848 annually. And many
of you have told me that you're getting a lot less than that. Whatever
we get, we are grateful for it. Without it, many of us would have no
income in old age at all.

In trying to make these funds last, some of us have been willing
to consider options outside our normal comfort zones. I met several
such women during my recent trip to San Miguel de Allende, Mexico, this little gem of a city and artists' enclave in the mountains and
high desert of central Mexico.

I first learned about San Miguel from Bonnie Lee Black (more on
her later), an American resident there, who connected with me around
a blog post I'd written. She told me she couldn't support herself in the
United States on her social security check of just under $1,000. On

the same money in San Miguel she could live comfortably. And she said she knew lots of older American women like herself who'd made the trek across the border for the same reason she had.

I made the trip to San Miguel to meet some of them. I interviewed six in depth and spoke with a dozen or so more. The women I interviewed are Americans in their fifties, sixties, and seventies, living on modest fixed incomes ranging from $650 to $2,300 per month. Some are recent arrivals to San Miguel and others have lived there a decade or more. All are reverse migrants from the States who did the math and figured, I can't make ends meet in the good ol' USA, and started looking for cheaper alternatives.

I come out of the working class, married at twenty-one, moved to the suburbs, i.e., Queens, and had three boys. The women's movement happened. I left the marriage and moved to Manhattan. I discovered there was something called a technical writer, later known as a documentation specialist. I worked on Wall Street in banking and brokerage firms earning the big bucks as a consultant. Once my sons were out on their own, I traveled between assignments. 9-11 happened. Zero jobs available. Went through my 401(k), which wasn't that much after putting the kids through college. Cash strapped, I moved in with a friend and then moved in with my mother, for which family members said I would receive sainthood. Serendipitously, ran into people who traveled the world teaching English and realized, I could do that! Moved to Mexico City. Mostly taught mid-level management business skills. At age sixty-two, took early social security and received little under $1,300. Twelve years ago I moved to SMA and, except for missing my grandkids, living happily ever after.

—Toni

I have nothing but admiration for these women who late in life ditched their possessions to make a fresh start. I am a veteran traveler myself, having visited Africa some fifty times (mainly for work) and as an army brat, moving fourteen times in twelve years to places like Italy, Germany, and Libya. But not once have I ever considered moving to a foreign country solo, and certainly not on my own steam without the backing and support of some government or corporate relocation department to do all the heavy lifting.

At seventy-one, I arrived in San Miguel to fulfill a wish on my bucket list. I landed and did not know a soul. After two weeks I quit my language class and just started wandering around. I still had a lease on a place in San Clemente, California. When I got back, I sold everything except for my cat, clothes and Engle carving knives. I am in my second year here in San Miguel and love my life. I support myself on the $1,800 I get in social security. I pay $600 a month for a two-bedroom, two-bathroom, completely furnished apartment plus a little garden. I am a little further from town than I want to be, but aside from that I live well. I couldn't afford to live the way I do here back in the States.

—Arianna

It takes guts to leave behind everything and everyone you know at any age, but especially in your fifties, sixties, and seventies. It's not for everyone, for sure. What my trip to San Miguel opened up for me, and maybe can for you, is the *possibility* of living overseas. That was not on my radar before. I am not saying I am moving to San Miguel or anywhere else, for that matter. I am saying it's no longer off the table. It's an option in my toolbox.

What changed my mind-set was how much the women I interviewed in San Miguel were like me and so many other women I know. I don't think any of them would describe themselves as particularly brave. I could see myself following in their path. After talking to them, their move to a foreign country no longer felt so "out there" as a decision.

I followed the script my parents wrote until the women's movement. That's when I realized I wasn't crazy for wanting to go a different way.

—Toni

I guess as a last resort I could have moved to some small town in Mississippi. Sure, it might be affordable, but I would've never been happy there; would have never fit in.

—Jade

Like many of us at this stage of life, the women I interviewed have zigged and zagged, doing a little bit of everything. There were burned-out entrepreneurs, corporate types who had been downsized, instructors, technicians, artists, and one homesteader. All arrived in San Miguel alone, never married or divorced, some with children and some without, some with good relationships with their adult offspring or works in progress, and some estranged for many years. There was more than one cancer diagnosis, and several cancer scares, and the surprise that our once "can-do-anything" bodies are slowing down with hip, knee, or back pain that none of us are quite used to yet.

I am used to just going, going, going. But it hurts when I stand up quickly now. I can't just pop up like I used to.

—Jade

I have lived in San Miguel for about five years now and feel part of a community here. No one ever visits from my old life back in the States. I have a boy and a girl in their fifties and sixties. We are not close and rarely communicate. Doesn't bother me at all.

—Cora

My trip to San Miguel was short, barely five days. Yet, I have been surprised how powerfully what I experienced there still resonates with me all these months later. Of course, I know that visiting a place is not the same as living there. Putting down roots somewhere always adds new layers of complexity. I learned that lesson as an army brat growing up overseas. Wherever my family was stationed in the world, we always lived in the local neighborhoods and not on base. When my dad went to Vietnam, my mom opted to continue living in Italy the year he was away rather than returning to the States as most spouses did.

That said, what I share about San Miguel below are just my first impressions after my short stay as a visitor.

I am smiling. I can't tell you how many people told me they visited for a week and ended up buying a house, later flying back to the States in stunned silence wondering what in the world they'd just done. It's that kind of place, if you have the money. I will be going back in the coming months for longer stays to see if it continues to hold the same magic for me.

Living in San Miguel is not the same as visiting. For one, this is a cash society. You can't just call up on the phone and pay your utility bill.

—Quinn

Every Day Felt Like Sunday

I am sure all who visit are struck by the sheer beauty of the place. I know I was. San Miguel is known for its near-perfect weather, cobblestone streets, lush gardens, and beautifully preserved baroque/neoclassical Spanish architecture. It is an old city and as such exists in a kind of time warp. The world seemed to slow down as I wandered the streets on foot. Every day felt like Sunday. I stayed in an Airbnb rental while I was there. I found that my mood lifted just walking out the front door. https://www.businessinsider.com/san-miguel-de-allende-voted-best-city-in-the-world-2017-7?r=UK&IR=T

My blood pressure has gone down since I moved here. I wish I had done it at sixty-five. I would have skipped a lot of financial mistakes, the Lexus, and all that pretending.

—Leah

Great Weather, Flat Shoes, and a Built-in Community

The older I get, the more I calibrate to the weather, and I loved the weather in San Miguel. It is situated some 6,200 feet above sea level, and being that high up keeps the temperature cool and dry if a little chilly some evenings and in the fall and winter months. I drank lots of water to stay hydrated and stave off altitude sickness. I walked most places, but cabs are cheap, about $3 to go anywhere in the city proper. Walking is quite a workout. The terrain is cobblestoned and hilly in places. I like my heels but will leave them at home on my next visit. And should you decide to visit, ditch the cute shoes for comfortable ones with ankle support, if possible, unless you want to become another one of the "fallen women of San Miguel."

There are only three months a year when the weather is not perfect.

—Jade

But it was more than the weather and architecture that called to me. There was a sense of community in San Miguel that I have not experienced in other places. People gather and keep up with each other. I heard story after story of help offered and received.

I was sick, and it was bad. I don't know how many days I had been in my apartment. I was hungry and wandered out into the street. I am sure I looked a mess. I saw a worker and asked him for a banana. I don't know why I asked for a banana, but that's what I wanted. He took one look at me and went and got a doctor. Doctors make house calls in San Miguel, so one came. The worker also went to my landlord, who not only organized my neighbors to bring me food but found a girl to do a little light housekeeping for me while I was down. And that worker, he stopped by to check on me every few hours for the next three days.

—Cora

In 2005, I spent the month of May in San Miguel. It was easy for a woman alone to navigate, easy to meet people. Everyone I met knew I'd just sold my brownstone in New York and was buying a house in New Orleans. After hurricane Katrina struck, I got an email from every one of them—are you all right, where are you staying? I was trying to figure that out. Winter was coming so I didn't want to go back to New York. My best friend in Atlanta was moving to London so I didn't want to stay there. I came back to San Miguel. I thought it was a nurturing place and that's what I'd need while I restored my house and figured out what to do next. I'd planned to stay eighteen months and am still here thirteen years later.

—Cynthia

I had a friend in denial about how badly she needed a hip replacement until one day she was literally holding on to buildings as she walked and then could not get down off the curb to cross the street. A guy on a motorcycle at a corner saw her predicament and asked if she needed help. He then proceeded to give her a ride home on his bike. Mexican people can be very kind.

—Toni

A Place to Call Home

Bonnie cooked a delicious chicken mole for me my first evening in San Miguel. It was great to finally meet her over a meal and a glass of wine. From her apartment window I could see across the city's skyline to the famous parish church, Parroquia de San Miguel Arcángel, known for its pink façade and wedding cake–like towers.

In the States we'd call Bonnie's apartment a studio, easily big enough for one person with a small kitchen and breakfast nook and space for a double bed. There was also a community terrace overlooking the city, where some neighbors hung their clothes to dry. And I noticed a washing machine in a little room off the courtyard on the ground floor.

Bonnie rents her apartment for $500 per month, including utilities, and could pay a lot less if she wanted to live farther out. But by living in the heart of the city, she's within walking distance of its thriving arts scene and other cultural attractions and amenities that matter to her.

Both Cynthia, sixty-eight, and Toni, seventy-four, moved to SMA some thirteen years ago from Atlanta and New York City, respectively. Both live within walking distance of the town center, Cynthia in a jaw-dropping four-story town house she rents for a song at $500 per month, and Toni in a very comfortable one-bedroom she rents for $370 per month including electricity.

There is no question that you can live in Mexico for a lot less than you can in the States: by half or more, depending on your lifestyle, according to one recent survey.[1] But extraordinary rent deals like the ones Cynthia and Toni got over a decade ago are not as easy to find today.

Those deals happened back in the days before *Condé Nast Traveler* dubbed San Miguel as the number one city in the world in 2013 and *Travel + Leisure* named it the best city in the world to visit in 2017. With those designations, it is no surprise that travelers are now flocking to SMA, driving up rental and real estate prices.

I am becoming one of those old women who shakes her broom and yells "Get off my lawn." I was spoiled by being here before all the tourism, big hotels, and exhaust-emitting SUVs that the Spaniards didn't plan for in their street design started flooding in.

—Toni

So, no question, prices are rising. But if you are living in a major metropolitan area in the United States and that's your benchmark, San Miguel is still very affordable.[2]

Freedom from Striving

What I really like about San Miguel is the freedom from striving. The Americans I interacted with did not seem to care about what I had done before. There were none of the usual "What do you do?" size-you-up–type questions. It was much more about who I am now and what I am focusing on in this phase of my life. I can't tell you what a relief it was to be away from all that jockeying and posturing for position. No one cared about what business I'd run or how big a budget I'd managed (or not) in my old life.

In the States your friends are ashamed of you because you don't have the right shoes. I don't have to fake it here.

—Cora

I also liked the pace of living. There's a lot to do without it being a rat race. There are music events, festivals, art exhibitions, cooking classes, and lectures. There are also a number of discussion groups formed around specific interests. There's a weekly salon for people interested in developments in science and another one for philosophy. A talk about the mind-body connection was the topic the week I was there.

In February, in honor of Black History Month, I attended a sold-out affair called "Black Voices" with readings from excerpts of famous black writers. San Miguel really is a cultural, intellectual, and artistic hub. It reminds me of one of those high-end continuing-care retirement communities affiliated with a major university, but at a tiny fraction of the cost.

We have a lot of speakers come through giving presentations. These are experts in their field. Some live here and others are on

179

vacation, often visiting every year. We listen to their talks and tear them apart. It's all in good fun.

—Cora

Those of us who have been here awhile have our projects, friends, and groups and tend to take less advantage of the cultural activities unless they fit in with our interests.

—Toni

And I found it an easy place to navigate. Mexico has gotten such a bad rap of late. Friends were afraid for me when I visited. I felt safe walking around in San Miguel. Of course, I remained alert as I would in any city. At night, I kept to the busy main streets and took cabs when the crowds thinned out.

I Am *Not* Invisible Here

I enjoyed seeing so many people my age on the streets of San Miguel. I liked the knowing glances, graying hair, and lined faces. It was a welcome break from my life in Washington, DC, where out and about I am often the oldest person in a sea of millennials.

Woman after woman mentioned feeling seen in San Miguel. Being old here had status. This was always shared with a little bit of amazement. In the States, it's not only that we're not young anymore; we're not anything. It's like we hit sixty and have dematerialized.

In San Miguel, you're nobody until you're eighty. I don't see well but am not invisible here. Motorists see me—are even watching out for me. Here, I am in no danger of being mowed down.

—Cora

Grandmothers play an important role in Mexican families; they are held up and revered. While in San Miguel, it was not uncommon to see elderly women walking arm in arm with their adult daughters, other family members forming a protective half circle around them.

> *San Miguel is a good place to be a woman. There's a tremendous respect for family, mothers, and older women.*
>
> —Bonnie

Many of the American women I met felt that this esteem for older Mexican women extended to all women. It was being a certain age (not nationality) that determined a woman's entry into this cherished circle.

What Happens if I Get Sick or Hurt?

Health care matters, especially at our age. And when weighing a move to a foreign destination, how good the health-care system is will be a make-or-break consideration. There are, of course, risks navigating an unfamiliar health-care system in a foreign country on a budget. But all the women I spoke with were comfortable with the health-care options in San Miguel.

What I write below is not meant to be a comprehensive overview of health care in Mexico. It is to share the experiences of a group of older American women who live there. Should you ever make such a move you would, of course, do your own deep dive, your own research. Each of us is different. Your decision would be based on your situation—general health status, preexisting conditions, family history, budget, etc.

Non-citizens who live in Mexico as foreign residents have access to two affordable health-care systems: public and private. Both offer a comprehensive range of medical services at a fraction of what they would cost in the United States. Local private hospitals, in town and in nearby cities like Queretaro, are equipped with the state-of-the-art technology and diagnostic equipment. Many of the doctors in the private system have studied or taken medical seminars abroad and are fluent in English. Several of the Americans I spoke with commented about their good bedside manner, as well as their willingness to make house calls (my mouth hit the floor when I heard that) and give out their cell phone numbers. Yet, costs in the private system are still shockingly low by American standards. A doctor's visit starts at $30 and goes up to $45 to $50 for a specialist. A house call would set you back $60 to $100, a colonoscopy $300, a mammogram around $100, and a hip-replacement $7,000 to $8,000.

If you are on a tight budget, there's the public health-care system which a number of the women I spoke with enlisted in for free through Seguro Popular, the government subsidized, need-based health-care insurance. Wait times in the public system are much longer and fewer physicians speak English, so unless you speak Spanish, you'll need to bring along a translator. Emergency room wait times in the public system are also long unless you arrive in an ambulance. And if you are admitted to a public hospital, you will need friends to assist you during your stay because, unlike in the United States, you will not be assigned a nurse or nurse's aide to take care of you.

That said, women who used the public sector medical facilities considered them a good affordable option (even if not as top-notch as the private system) and trusted the care they received for things like sprains and broken bones.

A friend cut the tip of her finger off in the blender and went to the emergency room, and they sewed it back on and charged her $8.

—Angela

My one experience using Seguro Popular was when I broke my arm. I spent eight days in the hospital waiting for the metal rod to be delivered from Leon. They admitted me because they don't always have a free bed, so I was saving my place. My arm was too fragile to travel to New York City, so I had the surgery done there. There are no nurses, so you have to have a friend or family member stay with you. There are no IV poles, just a hook hanging from the ceiling. So to go to the bathroom you have to unhook it, carry it with you, and hang it on a clothes hook in the bathroom. With one arm in a sling this was a challenge.

Then when I got back to New York City and saw an ortho-pedist to see if it was healed enough to take the rod out, he told me taking it out would do more damage and asked me why I let them put a rod in my arm. They haven't done that since WWII when they needed to get soldiers back into the field. But my arm is fine and fully functioning and it was done for free.

—Toni

Rods, WWII, what, what?—sounds maybe kind of dicey. I get it. But consider this: coverage for a year in the public system costs under $300 and often much, much less. And all I met who were enlisted described public health care in San Miguel as good to excellent.

I pay the equivalent of $54 per year for my Seguro Popular coverage and have no complaints.

—Bonnie

When I came here, the old timers told me not to worry about medical insurance, that if I put what I would have paid for my international policy in the bank, I would have enough to pay for any medical emergency that might arise. I was too afraid to do that, and now wish I had. I never used that insurance policy and would today have over $40,000 in the bank. That's what it cost *me over ten years. Now I have Medicare and Seguro Popular. Because my income is low and I don't own a house, I pay nothing.*

—Cynthia

There is no initial charge to enlist in Seguro Popular. You pay on a sliding scale based on your finances. The hospital will admit you with a tourist visa, which many people have because they come back and forth every six months to visit family. The care you receive on a tourist visa is cheap, but not free.

—Toni

There is also a wide variety of alternative therapies available in San Miguel: homeopathic and naturopathic doctors, acupuncturists, Chinese medicine, stem cell, etc., and all are very popular and much less expensive than in the United States. Acupuncture, I was told, costs between $20 and $50 per session. A visit to a naturopath will run you about $50, and stem cell therapy is available for $550.

I could never afford a naturopath in the United States, and the one I see here uses a sliding scale and admonishes you to not hesitate to see her even if you don't have money.

—Angela

I also heard of folks dipping back across the border by bus or plane to use their Medicare when they needed a specialist they couldn't find locally or who had too long of a waiting list in San Miguel.

I know in the back of my mind, and probably yours, too, that we're all worried about some catastrophic medical event wiping out what little savings we might have and totally uprooting our lives. Universal health care in San Miguel might not be perfect, but many I spoke with felt it spared them of that worry. And that's a big deal (even bigger if you're old enough to have Medicare as a backup).

Meet Bonnie

Bonnie wrote to me after reading one of my blog posts. I was intrigued by this woman, once a successful Manhattan caterer who, at fifty, in the mid-'90s, joined the Peace Corps to serve in Gabon, Central Africa, and, at seventy, retired to San Miguel de Allende, Mexico, for good.

Like many of us, Bonnie's had a cool casserole of a career doing work that interested her. She's been a well-paid writer/editor in corporate America, a self-employed caterer in New York, an economic development professional in Africa, an adjunct English professor, and an award-winning author of three published memoirs.

After a breast cancer scare, Bonnie checked off one more thing on her bucket list when she joined the Peace Corps. Foreign travel was not new to Bonnie, and her Peace Corps post in Gabon was not her first foray into Africa.

In her mid-twenties, she lived for three years in what was then Salisbury, Rhodesia (now Harare, Zimbabwe). Twenty-five years later she was back in Africa and so loved her work as a health and nutrition volunteer that she was not ready to return stateside when her two-year Peace Corps service was over.

"After Gabon, I wasn't ready to come back to the States, so I decided to extend my stay, traveling to Mali, West Africa, where I 'did my own thing,'" Bonnie told me, "creating an economic development project for women called the Patchwork Project."

She lived in Mali for two years and immersed herself in the culture, as she does everywhere she goes. "This is how we learn to love the world," she says. "Let a new place and new vista seep in slowly, over time. Learn the language (or give it a try!), eat the food, dance to the music."

No doubt Bonnie's experiences in Zimbabwe, Central Africa, and Mali have helped equip and prepare her for life in Mexico, not because the countries are the same. They're not, but the skill sets needed to live in culturally diverse nations, where English is not the first language, can be applied to other places.

Upon thinking about coming back to the States, Bonnie knew she didn't want to return to New York City and life in the fast lane. "I couldn't bear the thought of reentering the NYC rat race," she told me.

She ended up in northern New Mexico, where the slower pace appealed to her. But the job opportunities were limited. "I had to take early social security at sixty-two in order to survive. Without it, I just couldn't make ends meet," she said.

A dear friend lent her money to get her master's degree so that she could teach at the college level. With her MFA from Antioch-LA, she taught English and creative writing for ten years at the University of New Mexico–Taos.

She loved both teaching and her students, but, as an adjunct professor she made about $9 an hour, with no benefits. "It wasn't long before I realized I could no longer afford to live in the good ol' USA. Once you serve in the Peace Corps, you tend to think of the whole world as 'home,' so moving out of the US was not a difficult leap."

When I asked her why Mexico, she said: "I chose to live in Mexico where life is happy, slower, and less stressful, the cost of living lower, and my retirement savings, such as they are—after having supported myself as a single woman all of my adult life—might stretch farther. New Mexico is also a lot like Mexico. Coming here felt like the next lily pad over. It's close geographically and culturally. Mexico feels right to me now. The hard truth is that the US is a great country and a fine place to live if you have sufficient money. But if you don't, it's not."

Bonnie didn't just pick up and move blindly. She had visited San Miguel de Allende a couple of times before moving there, once attending a writers' conference in February 2015 and, on another occasion, house-sitting for a friend for four months. She also read many excellent books (easily obtainable at your library) on retiring to Mexico in general and on moving to San Miguel de Allende in particular. "It's important to do your homework," she told me.

Bonnie traveled light to Mexico. Like so many of us, she sorted through what to purge and what to keep. "I'd pick up items and stare them down. 'Can I live without you?' In most cases the answer was yes."

When I asked Bonnie if she has found community in Mexico, she said, "I meet many women in my age group—retired, divorced, former professionals—here who have similar stories. They discovered that they couldn't afford to live in the States. They learned about San Miguel de Allende, came here to check it out, fell in love with the place, and decided to retire here for good. To a woman, we are all deeply grateful to be here. We feel we've been given a new lease on life. I know I do. If I still lived in Taos, lovely as it is, I'd be eating cat food."

You can read more about Bonnie's life and adventures on her blog, The Wow Factor—Words of Wisdom from Wise Older Women: http://bonnieleeblack.com/blog.

Sharing Space and Our Lives

Remember to do the "Top This" exercise and to have three minutes of silence.

We boomers have never been a monolith. Our housing needs vary significantly, depending on a wide range of circumstances. But there's one common thread: housing is our biggest expense, and we've got to get that cost down as low as possible. The 30 percent rule of thumb tells us how much we can spend on housing. But let's say that we could spend up to 35 percent on it. Realistically, what would we have to work with, and what kinds of housing could we afford?

- ◆ What income can you count on, and for how long? Be brutal. We say that we're going to work well into our seventies, but is that realistic? Don't think about whether that's realistic for other people. Is that realistic for you?

- ◆ Is your current housing situation sustainable? How much of your income do you spend on living there? Can you see yourself paying this mortgage, rent, or condo fee? The utilities and other expenses year after year? Or are they kicking your ass now?

- ◆ If your housing costs were a third of what they are today, what would change in your life? What actions would you take that you're not taking now?

- ◆ How important is it to have an enormous roof over your head? How much of your current space do you actually live in? In other words, do you use all of the rooms in your home? Is living in a space much smaller than what you're used to something that you could consider or embrace?

- ◆ Have you and your friends been talking about living together in the same house or relocating to the same community? But beyond idle chitchat, these conversations go nowhere. What would it take to have this conversation in earnest? What questions do you need to ask yourself and one another? You have to start somewhere. Could you dedicate some time to this exploration over the next month? How about one hour of personal reflection and three hours engaging the individual or individuals with whom you might want to cohabitate?

• Does picking up and moving to another country intrigue you even a little bit? Or are you in the "You got to be kidding me" camp? If you wanted to go the next step in exploring this possibility, what could you do? You're not feeling Mexico but would be open to considering other overseas destinations. Check out https://international living.com/the-best-places-to-retire and https://www.liveandinvest overseas.com/best-places-to-retire for the best (and most affordable) places in the world to retire. Algarve, Portugal, has fascinated me since I learned how affordable and beautiful it is. For more information see http://money.usnews.com/money/blogs/on-retirement /2014/06/10/11-reasons-to-retire-in-portugals-algarve.

Chapter 11

Retirement Security Requires Housing Security

Affordable housing is not that affordable, and if it can be af-forded, there is a three- to five-year wait list.

—Jennifer

The majority of us live in our private residences with all of our possessions and more or less fend for ourselves. But this way of living is getting harder to keep up, as many of us in advanced middle age and older lack the resources to maintain our homes unassisted or to modify them to meet our evolving health needs. This is especially true for those of us with modest fixed incomes and with no friends or extended families to pitch in.

Affordable Housing: America's Big Denial Issue

The combination of reduced earnings in our later years, excessive housing costs, and lack of affordable options is at the root of the housing crisis. Government solutions have been slow to emerge, and the private sector has, to a great extent, focused on supplying the top end of the market, leaving millions of low- and moderate-income boomer households to fall through the cracks.

I am 61 and unemployed. Have downsized into a rented room in a friend's house. Wondering how to hang on long-term.

—Deborah

Tens of Millions of Us Are Living Longer on Less

With less income and little or no retirement savings, a staggering number of us are going to need affordable-living options—not just for a few years but for decades. Today there are 52 million Americans age sixty-five and older, but that number is dwarfed by the 82 million people between the ages of forty-five and sixty-four who are right behind them, many of whom will need suitable housing and aging support services too.

Thanks to advances in medical diagnosis and treatment, we can now expect to live longer, some of us well into our eighties. And that's the good news. The bad news is that millions of us will be financing this "longevity bonus" with smaller nest eggs.

According to AARP, "only one out of three older Americans receive regular payments from pensions and retirement savings."[1] With pensions pretty much going the way of the dinosaurs, we boomers are the first generation expected to save enough to fund our own retirement needs.

As we learned earlier, the retirement savings of the average household age 55 and up only generates about $310 in monthly income.[2] Kick in the average monthly social security benefit of $1,404 and you'll see where I'm going with this. Millions and millions of people have or will have *very* modest incomes. And where are we all going to live? When we apply the 30 percent rental rule to $1,651, we get $495 to put toward housing costs. And if we spend much more than that, we'll find ourselves scrimping on food and medicine to pay the rent. Many of us are accustomed to thinking about the affordable-housing crisis as some sort of inner-city problem. Not anymore.

Can what's happened to us change how we see other people across the board and create more empathy in us for "those people" who we'd have nothing in common with under other circumstances? Can we now look over at them instead of down on them? Do we see that the same systemic factors that deter-

mined their plight have now determined our own? Do we come out of this hardship feeling empathetic and connected, or do we stay in our zones of isolation?

—Marvin

Housing Costs Soar as Boomers' Incomes Fall

At the same time that boomers' incomes are shrinking, the costs of renting and buying homes are skyrocketing. Real Property Management, the largest residential property management franchise in North America, reports that housing costs have increased 2.4 percent per year over the last twenty years, while wages have been flat or falling. In a report on wage growth and home appreciation, housing expert RealtyTrac found that between 2012—the year the housing market bottomed out—and 2017, US median home prices have outpaced average weekly wage increases 69 percent to 9 percent over the period.[3]

Apartment rents, too, have gone through the roof. Apartment List analyzed census data from 1960 to 2014 and found that over this period "inflation-adjusted rents [rose] by 64 percent, but real household incomes increased by 18 percent."[4]

According to a 2014 study by Harvard's Joint Center for Housing Studies and AARP, one-third of Americans age fifty and over—or nearly 20 million households—were carrying a moderate or severe[5] housing cost burden, whereas in 2000 only one in four were. The study found that renters are twice as likely to be severely cost burdened as owners and that nearly half of all renters in the lowest income quartile are shelling out over 50 percent of their income on housing.

I was at the office when I got a call from a friend screaming that she was being evicted. The marshals were at her place at that very moment, throwing her stuff into garbage bags. I rushed over and sat guard over her things in the front yard as strangers in cars and pickup trucks drove slowly back and forth like vultures, seeing what could be had.

—Barry

And people of color are faring worse. The Harvard study found that older adults from ethnic and racial minorities are disproportionately burdened by housing costs, with Asian households spending 39 percent of household income on housing, Hispanic households spending 43 percent, and black households spending 46 percent, compared to 29 percent for whites.

No Relief in Sight

America's affordable-housing crisis is a classic supply-and-demand problem. There just isn't enough affordable housing for all of the people who need it. And the gap is widening as growing numbers of boomers on low or moderate fixed incomes flood the market with insufficient resources to cover their housing costs.

It needs to be stressed that a significant source of the problem is the skyrocketing cost of housing over the past thirty plus years. When I was growing up in the '70s, even a lower-middle-class salary such as my mother's could support an entire family. We sold our duplex in Boston for $36,000. Last year, another duplex on the same small, cramped street was listed for $1.1 million. Meaning, even if you deducted $1 million from the price of that house, it would still be three times what we sold our house for.

—Charles

How big is the gap? According to Erika Poethig, Urban Institute's director of urban policy, "For every 100 households with incomes at or below 30 percent of the area median income, there are only 28 affordable units available, down from 33 in 2007 and 37 in 2,000 . . . The situation has gotten so out of whack that there's not a single county in the entire country where supply of affordable rental property meets demand."[6]

And this is still true today. According to a June 2018 report from the National Low Income Housing Coalition, a full-time minimum wage worker cannot afford a modest two-bedroom apartment anywhere in the country.[7] No wonder we're reading news accounts about people waiting years for a handful of slots in rent-regulated apartment buildings. Winning the lottery might be easier.

Apartments are so tight that when someone's grandmother dies, the first thing that pops into your mind is "Does she live in a rent-controlled building?" Rude, I know.

—Byron

There's a big demand and a big opportunity, so you'd think that the private sector would be jumping in and that developers would be salivating over the opportunity to build millions of affordable rental units. But the economics of affordable housing is hard. Development costs are high, and it's not easy to cover those costs and to make a profit when tenants are paying such low rents. According to experts, "the gap between the amount a building is expected to produce in rents and the amount developers will need to pay lenders and investors can stop affordable-housing development before it even begins."[8]

Government participation is needed to make the numbers work. But the tax incentives and fiscal policies that are in place have not come close to inducing the production of enough low-income units to close the housing affordability gap.

The government agencies and housing advocates who grapple with these issues daily understand what's at stake. The hitch is that they face strong headwinds on Capitol Hill. Budget cuts and changing priorities have led to reduced federal·funding for vouchers and other housing programs. In fact, housing assistance currently serves only 24 percent, or about one out of four, of the 19 million eligible households.[9]

For us boomers, the upshot of all of this is that no fairy god-mother is coming to the rescue. It will take years, if ever, to solve the affordable-housing crisis. That means that, despite long waits, we apply for the government programs that we're eligible for but know that ultimately it is on us to take matters into our own hands and to look after ourselves and one another.

Let's give kudos to Chris Hawkins at Senior Living, who's done the "deep dive" on Department of Housing and Urban Development (HUD) programs that offer rent assistance, support for home ownership, and services that help older adults and persons with disabilities. You can find information about eligibility requirements and how to apply here: http://www.seniorliving.org/lifestyles/hud-senior-housing-programs.

Living on a Tight Budget

Don't clutter your life with stuff you cannot afford. Keep your overhead low. Get a car with good mileage. Work toward buying your apartment. Shop at Gap. Enough with obsessing over the latest bag. It's a purse. It holds stuff. Get a backpack. You're being ridiculous.

—Sarah Silverman

Even if we're strapped for cash, we have options for how and where we live. We can take in housemates to defray expenses, move in with our parents or adult children in multigenerational homes, consider tiny homes, move into some kind of co-sharing arrangement, "small up" to more affordable conventional homes, do reverse mortgages and stay put where we are, or relocate to less expensive cities or countries. Like the group of American women we just met, all in their sixties or older, who decided they could no longer afford to live in the States and moved to San Miguel de Allende, Mexico.

Now, if we're secretly harboring fantasies about going back to our nice little lives in 1998, with our good jobs and disposable incomes, we're probably not going to like any of the above options. If we're starting to get our brains around the changes that are happening, maybe we can begin to focus on what's ahead instead of what's behind us. Will we get everything we want? Nope, and in some cases not by a long shot. Can we pull forward into the future the things that really matter to us? I think that that's more of a possibility— although we may not be able to take every little thing. Let's work on achieving the big things for now.

Housing is the single biggest expense in our "unretirement," often taking an even bigger bite out of our budgets than health care. If your finances are dicey, keeping a roof over your head is your top priority. We've all heard of the "homeless" friend couch surfing at his brother's place or living with one of his adult children. We're hoping not to have to do that.

I was let go from my job in 2014 and ended up crashing at my thirty-two-year-old daughter's place for seventeen months.

—Samantha

If housing is our biggest expense, then getting that cost down as low as possible has to be among our top priorities. A friend shared that someone she knew lowered his housing costs so much that he could cover them by working just four days per month. Now, that's what I'm talking about. I know that we all say that we're going to work well into our seventies. But really? Some of us are already tired, especially if our work histories involve arduous physical activity (e.g., work in the construction trades). Some of us will confront health issues that will prevent us from working in our later years.

Might "live low to the ground" become our new mantra? Getting our fixed costs down as far as possible will buy us freedom. When I think of making a purchase, I think about how long I'm going to have to work to pay for it. I'm not trying to live life in a hurry. I want pauses in my days so that I can engage with the people and things that matter to me. I want to be free. I am not free if I have to spend all my time working to pay off a bunch of stuff. Talk about stuff. My mouth hit the floor when I learned there are more than 50,000 self-storage facilities in the United States. To put that number in perspective, there are twice as many storage facilities as there are Starbucks and McDonald's combined.

Before we look at some of these housing options, let's look at two big trends that affect how and where we live: one-third of us are single—as in never married, widowed, or divorced—and we'd prefer to "age in place" or at least "in our community."

More Boomers Are Aging Alone

Growing numbers of boomer-aged Americans are "alone." We got here in all kinds of ways: some never married, some divorced, and some became widows or widowers. According to a study that appeared in the *Gerontologist*, one-third of Americans between the ages of forty-five and sixty-three are single; that number is up 50 percent since 1980.[10] And 9.2 million of the noninstitutionalized older adults living alone are women, which is more than twice the number of men living alone (4.1 million).[11]

It used to be that older unmarried Americans were mainly widowed or divorced. That's changed over the years. Today the majority of them are divorced or never married. Widowers only account for 10 percent of older single people.

The study found that unmarried boomers pay a high price for their singlehood in terms of negative economic, social, and health impacts. Now, I recognize that if you're older, single, and doing OK—or even better than OK—this finding may be a little grating. I know I cringed when I read it. There's a difference between being broke and being broken.

But according to the researchers, more and more boomers are living alone, and the number of people experiencing loneliness and isolation is also going up. And this has implications for our housing. Many of us who have lived alone for a long time have never even considered whether it's the best option for us going forward. It's just what we've always done. But the question now is: Does this way of living still serve us?

Many of us are not making new friends, are cut off from old friends, and live far from our extended families. We've gotten used to rowing our own little canoes. Privately, some of you have told me that you miss social interactions and ache with loneliness but don't know what to do about it.

We know that we humans are inherently social creatures. The quality and quantity of our social relationships really do matter. And the truth is that we are more cut off and isolated than before. A study by two Brigham Young University researchers found that there has been "a threefold increase in the number of Americans who say they have no close confidantes."[12]

> *Everyone has had a relationship that made a difference. When a relationship goes well, we can see the benefit. For some of us, that memory has faded. Somehow we've drifted away, and our souls ache. We don't want to talk about the weather. We want a deeper connection—a sense of social fabric. Wouldn't it be great if we could build that?*
>
> —Adam

Numerous studies show that chronic feelings of loneliness and isolation have "an impact on health comparable to the effect of high blood pressure, lack of exercise, obesity or smoking"[13] and are "on par with other known risk factors for cardiovascular disease such as anxiety and job strain."[14] Researchers have coined the term *elder orphans* to describe aging boomers without adult children, spouses, or companions to rely on. Dr. Maria Torroella Carney, MD, the chief of geriatric and palliative medicine at North Shore–LIJ Health System, estimates that "nearly one-quarter of Americans over age 65 are currently or at risk to become 'elder orphans.'"[15]

We know that living alone as we age impacts our finances. But we're learning that being single and childless by chance or choice can also have repercussions for our health. That's not something that we thought much about when we were young. Older now and living alone, we're wondering how we're going to take care of ourselves if we get sick or need help with daily living. Typically, family caregivers are the first line of support. But what happens if we don't have families, or families that we can count on?

I fall into that no-kids, never-married camp. I have a brother and have always felt very close to my two nieces. But I was on my own during my bout with breast cancer. My family just was not there for me. Facing that alone was deeply hurtful. I'm still not over it.

—Vivian

And there is a good reason to worry about not having a good support system. According to the Family Caregiver Alliance, "50 percent of elderly who have long-term care needs but no family available to care for them are in nursing homes, while only 7 percent who have a family caregiver are in institutional settings."[16]

I live alone. At fifty-eight, I had open-heart surgery. Anyone who's been through that knows how steep a climb the recovery is. I have a big, loving family, but my friends live closer to me. Everyone chipped in, bringing me food, cleaning my apartment, doing laundry, and running errands. It was an intense four or five months before I could even begin to take care of myself. I think about what would happen if I ever needed long-term care. There are limits to what you can ask of your friends.

—Taylor

Many of us who have lived alone for a long time cannot imagine sharing our homes with other people and cannot get our brains around taking in boarders. Even cohousing seems like a stretch. This is not to say that every older adult who lives alone is lonely. But if we are lonely, shouldn't sharing our homes be on the table as we consider our futures, especially now that we know that being lonely and cut off from social connections puts our health at risk? None of us can afford to wait until we're frail and dependent on others to start trying to put a plan together.

One way to start is to engage in conversations with people who are grappling with the same issues and concerns that we are. The Elder Orphans Facebook group is a supportive community that you can join if you want camaraderie and practical advice on a range of topics related to aging well and independently. You will find the group here: https://www.facebook.com/groups/elderorphans.

Also check out Villages (http://vtvnetwork.org), a membership-driven, grassroots organization of like-minded older adults committed to helping one another age in place in their homes/communities. Operated by volunteers and paid staff, Village members support each other in neighborhood-centric groups and benefit from coordinated access to affordable services, including transportation, health and wellness programs, home repairs, shopping discounts, and social and educational activities and outings. There are currently 200 Villages and another 150 or so under development in 45 states and the District of Columbia.

We Want to Age in Place, but Can We Afford It?

When the Demand Institute asked 4,000 baby-boomer households between the ages of fifty and sixty-nine where they wanted to retire, 63 percent said they planned to continue living in their current residences.[17] In an AARP study on the same topic, 87 percent of adults age sixty-five and older said they planned to stay in their homes.[18]

Still active and independent, we may not yet be too concerned about aging in place—and about whether we can pay for it. Too often it takes a health issue to focus our attention.

My stay in rehab after my hip-replacement surgery was extended eight days because I live alone, could not drive, and had no one at home to help me navigate my apartment.

—Michelle

It's important to think about accessibility, too, especially because 70 million of us over fifty have already developed at least one chronic health condition or had a major health event. In our late fifties and early sixties, it's not too soon to be thinking about whether our current living situations can meet our needs as we age and about how to make and pay for needed modifications (if we decide that that's the direction we want to go in).

You know you're getting old when you take your father to the movies and you both qualify for senior discounts.

—Brandon

While growing numbers of us say that we want to age in place, very few of our homes were designed with the kind of age-friendly features that would allow us to grow old in them safely and comfortably. A 2016 Harvard study found that just 3.5 percent of the US housing inventory was outfitted with all five universal design features that make homes accessible to people with impaired mobility or other physical or cognitive limitations. These features include single-floor living, inlcuding a ground-floor bedroom and bathroom with grab bars and no-skid surfaces, wide doorways and halls that can accommodate wheelchairs, lever-style door handles, and no-step accessible entry ways.

The extensive renovations needed to retrofit homes with these kinds of age-friendly amenities are not cheap. Affluent seniors may have the resources to pay for them out of pocket, but that's likely not the case for those of us in low- and even middle-income households.

I get it. Money is tight. Thinking about aging in place is just not a priority right now. But here's what you don't want: you don't want to have some health emergency down the road and risk a premature stay in an assisted living or nursing care facility because you live alone, can't get around in your own home, and don't have easy access to the support services you need.

Senior Resource is an excellent place to begin our exploration of aging in place. It's just chockablock full of information and lots of links to other sites: http://www.seniorresource.com/ageinpl.htm #resource.

Below are some options for "age-proofing" our homes on tight budgets.

You'll see that there are numerous government and nongovernment programs that offer financial assistance and support to low- and moderate-income older adults who want to make home modifications and repairs so that they can age in place. Unfortunately, not every state has these kinds of programs, but many do. The Paying for Senior Care website is a robust one-stop shop that will tell you everything you need to know about how to access not only these home-modification programs but also the full range of life-span care services. To get started, try the website's resource locator tool, which will help you sort through the maze of program eligibility requirements and give you a basic understanding of what support is available in your area.

And if you don't need this yet for yourself, you can always file it away.

Here are three additional Web pages to check out:

https://www.payingforseniorcare.com/home-modifications/state -assistance-programs.html

https://www.payingforseniorcare.com/home-modifications/how-to -pay-for-home-mods.html

https://www.payingforseniorcare.com/medicaid-waivers/wa-community -first-choice.html

And here's a final note: I know that some of you live in states without these kinds of programs. Others don't qualify because you don't yet meet the minimum age requirement or because you have incomes that are above the government-mandated low-income threshold but not high enough to afford to pay market rates. I know it's frustrating, but without a comprehensive solution to the senior-housing crisis, we who are experiencing it right now have to cobble together solutions as best we can.

My Aging-in-Place Story

I want to age in place, but not where I currently live. I love my home and neighborhood. I bought my home thirty-five years ago when the park across the street was considered too dangerous for an evening stroll. Today it hosts my favorite drumming circle and people pushing nice strollers, on yoga mats, or drinking iced lattes.

Prices have skyrocketed in the three-plus decades I've lived here. I wouldn't have a prayer of buying in this neighborhood today.

As much as I like my place, I don't see it as my forever home. When I moved in at age twenty-nine, I liked that it was on two floors. At sixty-four, I still see the sixteen steps up to my bedroom as good exercise. At seventy-four, I probably won't.

In fact, my house—aside from some grab bars in the shower—has none of the universal design elements that would make it conducive to aging in place. There's no bed or bath on the main floor. The corridors and doorways are too narrow to accommodate a wheelchair. My doors have knobs instead of lever handles. And forget zero-step entrances. You've got to walk up a flight of steps just to ring the doorbell.

So, while I don't have to move tomorrow, I likely will have to at some point unless I want to convert my small dining room into my bedroom. And I don't want to do *that* if I can help it. We've all been in homes where that was the family's only option for taking care of an older relative with mobility challenges.

Fixing the small stuff to age in place is generally not the problem. We can remove trip hazards and scrape together money to add extra lighting, install grab bars or an elevated toilet seat. The problem is when we can't afford more costly modifications needed to live safely and independently in our homes, like a chairlift or room addition for single-level living. That's when we're stuck. It really is a quality-of-life issue.

I got my chairlift through a local advocacy organization that helps seniors. At first, I just used it to take my groceries up the steps and occasionally to transport a suitcase. I use it all the time now, since I've been having all this trouble with my hip. I can't manage the stairs without it.

—Denise

Last year my own mother decided she was ready to downsize and leave behind the family home she'd lived in for forty-five years. That home with its four stories and five bedrooms had become too much to manage. That and "too many steps" convinced my mother it was time to move to a smaller place all on one floor.

Working with a senior living referral agent, I accompanied my mother on tours of independent and assisted-living facilities, visiting nearly a dozen. I was curious about their offerings myself, wondering if I, too, might end up in one one day. Here was an opportunity to learn alongside my mother.

I already knew they could be pricey, based on accounts of friends, but *jaw-dropping* is the word I'd use. Some of these places reminded me of cruise ships on land. I am not saying they weren't beautiful or that having my mother live in one wouldn't have given me peace of mind. I just also learned to brace myself for sticker shock whenever a tour guide described a sitting area with a fancy coffee dispenser as "the bistro." What that signaled is that the monthly service package had just shot up from $5,500 to $8,500 or more.

And don't get me started on the six-figure entry fees, bundled services, and other add-ons. I did not see one unit that was remotely affordable even for a middle-market customer and forget about the tens of millions of boomers in financial jeopardy. My mother, who, sadly died in March of last year, had my father's pension, some savings, and social security benefits. She owned a home and had other real estate. And it was going to take every bit of all of that to swing the costs long term.

As I toured one continuing-care retirement community after another, I wondered who the customer of the future would be. Who is going to plunk down a six-figure entry fee and pay nearly $4,000 in monthly maintenance charges? It won't be us boomers in our fifties and sixties who are approaching old age with more debt, little savings, and no pensions.

No wonder so many of us aspire to age in place. No one I know can afford to live in one of these continuing-care cruise ships. Even friends who can don't want the fortress-like setting, age segregation, regimented meal plans, and other bundled services.

We boomers are not our parents.

No Stampede for Affordable Housing

Remember that 1950's sitcom *Leave It to Beaver*? Well, things have changed a lot since then, when 43 percent of American households were nuclear families (defined as a married couple with children under eighteen). Today, nuclear families account only for 20 percent of households. The biggest household category, at 28 percent, is actually single people living alone; followed by couples without children, 25 percent; and adults living together, 20 percent.[19] This is a seismic shift when you think about it. Nearly half of American households are made up of adults living alone or adults sharing living space with other adults.

But when we look at existing US housing stock, there's a big mismatch between what's available and what people need given these changes in household demographics. Nearly 40 percent of US housing stock (39.82 percent) have three bedrooms, 26.54 percent have two bedrooms, 16.66 percent have four bedrooms, 11.63 percent have one bedroom, and 4.48 percent have five bedrooms.

Put another way, there are about half as many one-bedroom units as there are two-bedroom units even though singles living alone make up the biggest number of households. In fact, nearly 60 percent of the US housing stock has three or more bedrooms. And most, even the biggest houses, were designed for 1950s-style nuclear families with a master bedroom for the parents and smaller bedrooms for the kids.

When we add to this basic supply and demand problem what we already know about rising home prices, escalating rents, and flat and falling wages, we see why we're in such a housing bind. Housing costs are going through the roof when median income is barely budging. And the demand by diverse households for new and affordable types of housing is not being met by the available housing stock.

While there is no stampede to build affordable housing for this new America including older Americans in financial jeopardy, some home builders, developers, planners, and policy makers are already thinking more creatively about how to address the affordable housing crisis facing many older Americans in financial hardship. They are testing and scaling a wider range of affordable housing options. And they are rethinking innovation priorities as being much more than incorporating bistros, rooftop terraces, and shinier stainless steel appliances into new senior housing facilities.

Rethinking Small

Keeping in mind that nearly half of American households today are made up of one or two people, we need more initiatives like the new housing model MAGIC (multi-ability/multigenerational, inclusive community), from senior solutions pioneer Bill Thomas. Featuring the MINKA tiny house, MAGIC comprises "small homes built through modular construction, using technological advances to minimize costs."[20]

The smallest Minka house is 325 square feet in size and is fully accessible under the Americans with Disabilities Act guidelines. This is a big deal. ADA compliance (and the more comprehensive Universal Design) is uncommon in tiny house construction even though buyers age fifty and up constitute 40 percent of the market.

What I like about Minka is that it takes a fundamentally different approach to how homes are designed and constructed. It's a departure from convention not just in terms of size, but in its use of the "latest advances in digital design tools, robotics, and construction materials to minimize costs."

Minka, at a cost of $60,000 to $75,000 per unit, is not cheap, but it costs much less than the $300,000 median price of a home in the United States today. It's a viable option for young people who've been shut out of the housing market, where even starter homes are pricey and out of reach. And for empty-nesters in their sixties and older who don't want the headache or expense of maintaining a large, multilevel family home, Minka can mean the difference between living independently and being forced into residential care.

So, yes, we want to age in place, but we also want many more choices about where and how we do it. Minka is one option. We need many more.

Reimagining Obsolete Spaces

I am also intrigued by the growing interest in reinventing obsolete spaces: decommissioned schools, shuttered motels, vacant office buildings, and the like. Typically, what we see are vacant and abandoned buildings turned into luxury apartments and boutique hotels. That's why I was impressed with the New Jersey–based nonprofit and real estate developer Build with Purpose, whose mission is to convert convents and other empty buildings into affordable housing for low- and moderate-income seniors and other vulnerable populations.

Churches all over the country are grappling with what to do with convents that are now empty or underutilized. The last fifty years have witnessed a precipitous drop in the number of nuns in the United States, from a high of about 180,000 to under 47,000 today.[21] With few young recruits entering the convent, the average Roman Catholic sister is now about seventy-four years old.

Build with Purpose is among the nonprofit housing advocacy organizations thinking creatively about how to make use of these sacred spaces and turn them into community assets. It spent $1.1 million to convert the vacant 17,000-square-foot St. Peter the Apostle convent in River Edge, New Jersey, into affordable housing for older adults. The St. Peter the Apostle Senior Residence opened its doors in April 2013 and is now home to twenty-five residents.

The twenty-five-unit facility includes private bedrooms with shared bathrooms, a shared kitchen, a dining room, a community living and activity room, and other common areas. Conversions can be expensive, but this one was not. Because the former convent was already designed for communal living, it could be refurbished and restored at a relatively modest price. Build with Purpose founder and president Brian Keenan estimates that new construction of the same facility would have cost over $5 million.

With rents starting at $1,900, the St. Peter the Apostle Senior Residences costs less than half what a traditional assisted living facility costs in New Jersey, even though it offers many of the same services. I know, I know, I too still get a little sticker shock at these prices. This is, after all, close to what we think of as dorm living—very nice dorm living, but still dorm living. It helps that it is all-inclusive, so everything is covered. But I hear you. It's still out of reach for many.

Of course, neither the Minka project nor these convent conversions are "the" answer to the affordable senior housing crisis. I mention them to give you an idea of some of the initiatives in the works.

Pushing the Boundaries in Continuing Care

Before getting into house sharing options, I want to circle back to continuing care.

At this age, we're not easily impressed, but I must say, I was bowled over when I visited Aldersgate, a senior living and life plan community in Charlotte, North Carolina. Located on a beautiful 231-acre natural campus complete with trails and water features, it's the first time I thought, *Wow, if I had the money, I would live here.*

I single out Aldersgate not because of its affordability. It caters to an affluent customer and offers all the high-quality services and lifestyle amenities one would expect in such a setting. What's unique about Aldersgate and what intrigued me is the way it is facing head-on the market changes confronting continuing-care retirement communities and reinventing itself accordingly in ways big and small. It has found a way to maintain its status as a high-end provider while at the same time proactively engaging and supporting its lower-income neighbors in the East Charlotte community just outside its gates.

Four years ago, Aldersgate, at both the board and executive leadership levels, made a decision to change fundamentally its relationship with the surrounding community. Moving away from what had traditionally been an us-versus-them relationship, Aldersgate today seeks to connect with its neighbors and leverage the gift of its geography to positively impact youth, family, and senior living in East Charlotte.

Aldersgate understood that a change of this magnitude could not happen without extensive consultation. And it committed the time and resources to make it happen, meeting with city planners, local neighborhood associations, and community partners. Aldersgate also sought input from its own residents,[22] staff, and neighbors through numerous Story Circles. Through these circles it was able to identify the community's needs and desires based on input from the people who actually lived there. All of this feedback informed Aldersgate's overall master site planning and development, including consideration of more diverse price point housing on its campus to support older adults at a variety of income levels and Aldersgate staff with family workforce lodging.

This mission to be a good neighbor, amplify marginalized voices, and play a leading role in invigorating the surrounding East Charlotte community shows up in a number of concrete programs and initiatives. For example, Aldersgate has joined forces with Carolina Farm Trust on an initiative called Urban Farm at Aldersgate. This 6.7-acre working farm and learning center aims to expand the healthy food options for food-insecure families living in Charlotte's east side.

Aldersgate also helps seniors living off its campus by providing meals to the local PACE program. It offers services to neighborhoods nearby through the Aldersgate at Home program, dedicated to providing reliable and cost-effective care in a home setting. And it has teamed up with a neighboring Title 1 school, University of North Carolina at Charlotte, as well as the Jewish Community Center and residents of Aldersgate to conduct a summer literacy program for children.

Aldersgate has also been designated one of the first platinum-level SAGECare-certified organizations in the country, with over 95 percent of its more than 500 employees having successfully completed LGBTQ cultural competence training.

Aldersgate is reimagining what a continuing-care retirement community can be and can look like. It need not be a fortress. It can actively seek out and engage diverse communities and be a good neighbor. It can explore new models of affordability. It can provide meaningful opportunities for its residents to make a difference through purposeful engagement. And it can extend its offerings to include in-home care services for seniors who wish to age in place.

The takeaway for me is that even if you are a high-end facility, you can use your economic muscle in more than token ways for the betterment of the community where you reside.

House Sharing as a Strategic Response

I had the perfect housemate. She came home, didn't talk to me, and went straight to her room. She never cooked or had people over, and she paid in advance. I barely noticed she was there.

Now, this might not be what everyone wants, but it worked out great for me.

—Dee

Many of us are unemployed, underemployed, or—in the feast/famine world of contract work—trying to pay high fixed housing costs with wages that are unreliable and bouncing all over the place. Or we're on fixed incomes, making a fraction of what we used to make, with our housing costs taking big bites out of our money. Under these circumstances, we may be more receptive to house sharing as a way to stabilize our incomes and cut expenses.

Seven out of ten boomers own homes, and many of us have seen the market come back in recent years after the pummeling it took in 2008. Even after refinancing in the past, we still have equity in our homes, but our earning power is not what it used to be. Cash poor and house rich, we can turn to house sharing, which can provide supplemental incomes and help us keep our homes if we're at risk of losing them.

Some of us, of course, have not seen the housing market recover and may still be upside down in our homes. House sharing can ease the financial pressures we're under and allow us to bide our time until prices (hopefully) rebound in part or full in our areas.

Of course, a lot of us are renting and are sharing or open to sharing our apartments/homes too.

And if we're empty-nesters, we might share our places for companionship or out of necessity to help pay the bills and keep a roof over our heads. And home sharing need not always involve the exchange of money. For example, some people provide accommodations in exchange for help with meals, transportation, housework, and the like.

Two can live cheaper than one. I have a contact, a friend of a coworker, who needs a room. I'm seriously considering a boarder. I have an empty furnished bedroom with a bathroom,

since my daughter is older and has moved out (so it's a delight-
ful room for a gal). I must think outside the box these days.

—Janet

Now, finding the right house or apartment mate can be a dicey proposition. We're all worried about having an ax murderer move into our homes, or a deadbeat whom we can't get rid of. And sometimes we love our friends but can't live with them, and in order to house share, we'd need to find the right strangers.

The National Shared Housing Resource Center (http://national sharedhousing.org) is a clearinghouse for people who are looking for shared-housing support organizations in their communities to help them find a housemate. It's different from some other roommate-finding sites in that its focus is on mature adults. Please check out the NSHRC's resource directory for state listings. Many of the organizations mentioned here have staff members who will help you screen potential housemates through interviews, background checks, and personal references.

CoAbode (http://www.coabode.org) is a community for single mothers to share housing resources and support. I include CoAbode on this list because "life happens" and more than one of you have told me that you have ended up having custody of your grandchildren and could use some support. Or maybe you have an adult daughter who could benefit from this resource.

The Golden Girls Network (http://goldengirlsnetwork.com/about -golden-girls-network/) helps like-minded single women and men who are looking for affordable places to live through senior home sharing.

Nesterly (https://www.nesterly.io/), winner of the 2017 NYC BigApp Competition, is really an old-school concept gone digital. Dubbed "the Airbnb of affordable housing," Nesterly is a platform for intergenerational home sharing. It matches young people who need affordable housing with older adults who have affordable space/rooms to rent in their homes and will discount rent for help with chores.

Silvernest (https://www.silvernest.com/share-house) is a unique roommate matching service for boomers and empty-nesters with space to share. It offers assistance with things like lease agreement preparation and how to set up online rent collection.

In her book *Sharing Housing: A Guidebook for Finding and Keeping Good Housemates*, Annamarie Pluhar offers some excellent tips and useful guidelines for sharing living spaces. Pluhar has lived in shared housing for over twenty years and is also available for consultations if you're considering shared living but need hands-on help to get started.

> *My friends who have lost their jobs cannot find employment. We all know that it's thanks to ageism. My best friend and I always said we would live together as old women. We aren't there yet, but soon. It won't be easy. Her lifestyle is about as different from mine as I can imagine, and she shows very few signs of flexibility. But I continue to think that we women must think of sharing housing as young people do so that we can avoid facing being homeless. I admit that I am scared.*
>
> —Robin

And finally, if you're interested in rent-free house sitting and caretaking opportunities, check out *The Caretaker Gazette* (www.caretaker.org). First published in 1983, this subscription-based newsletter posts hundreds of new jobs each year in the US and overseas. Other companies that match homeowners with house sitters include MindMyHouse (https://www.mindmyhouse.com) and HouseCarers.com (https://www.housecarers.com).

Two or More Generations Living under One Roof

A big trend in the housing market is the movement toward multigenerational homes. These are homes that can accommodate the needs of two or more generations. Their designs include common areas and private spaces, and some have self-contained generation suites, or "casitas." According to one online brochure, the aim is to "[keep] everyone together, but comfortably apart."

I have always been intrigued by multigenerational homes. I wondered whether one could work for my own family. My dad died a decade ago, and my mother, who recently died, continued to live in the family home. But four levels and five bedrooms was too much for her, and she often talked about wanting to move into a small one- or two-bedroom apartment that would be easier to manage. That got me thinking about the privacy suites in these "multigen" homes. I take care of my grandson two nights a week and thought that maybe my daughter could also move in.

I've lived in my current home for thirty-five years, and although I'm cash poor, I've built up substantial equity. In a plan I had before my mother died, my mom and I would both sell our homes, pool our resources, and find a multigenerational residence in Washington, DC. But I learned that my mom would prefer suburban Virginia, where she could be near her friends, and I can't imagine living outside of the city I've lived in for decades. I could also tell she was not keen on the so-called privacy suite, which someone called a "granny pod," lessening its appeal. Meanwhile, my daughter had met someone.

So you see how many variables there are to consider.

When I was looking at multigenerational homes, many that I saw were located a little farther out than I would have liked, but that's just me. We boomers are a diverse bunch. I want urban living with walkable streetscapes, neighborhood-serving stores, and other amenities, but someone else could just as legitimately want to be off the grid and close to nature.

I still love the multigenerational-home concept, but my family's brief flirtation with it should give you an idea of all of the ducks that have to be in a row for it to work.

Multigenerational Households on the Rise

Multigenerational households have long been common in some immigrant communities where cultures and traditions support the idea of an extended family living together under one roof. But the hard economics of the great recession—including foreclosures, job losses, underemployment, and rapidly rising student debt—caused families across all demographics to start looking at the benefits of pooling resources.

> *I was at a dinner recently and this woman of Italian descent mentioned that her twenty-seven-year-old son was still living at home. The Americans immediately started in on her with the "failure to launch" talk. She pushed back, asking what was wrong with her son living at home. He worked, was responsible, and contributed to the family. She didn't understand why we Americans assign so much status to living independently. What, so we can all have our own lawnmowers and snowblowers?*
>
> —Diane

According to Pew Research, the number of multigenerational households (i.e., those including at least two adult generations) in the United States increased from 46.6 million, or 15.5 percent, in 2007 to 64 million, or 20 percent, in 2016.[23] A study conducted by the National Association of Realtors found that the two biggest reasons that people purchased multigenerational homes were to save money (24 percent) and because children over the age of eighteen were returning home (24 percent).[24] Those who buy these homes are often between the ages of forty-nine and fifty-eight (22 percent) and sixty-six and eighty-eight (18 percent).

With so many unmarried boomers, one-quarter of whom live with adult children who often have children of their own, it's obvious why the demand for multigenerational housing is growing. Married and cohabitating boomers are also consolidating households to cut costs, having elderly parents move in, and living under one roof with "boomerang" children who are marrying later.

Building Codes and Ordinances Are Still Headaches

Multigen homes represent a multifaceted response to this doubling-up trend, and new housing designs accommodate the lifestyles and living preferences of multiple generations. They run the gamut in design and price. You can choose from affordable and small (under six hundred square feet) accessory dwelling units (ADUs) that can be attached to conventional single-family houses or stand on their own in the backyard, to starter castles with $2 million price tags made by home designers like Jeffrey Collé.

Multigen homes are considered a new type of housing, and in many jurisdictions local ordinances, zoning laws, and codes have yet to catch up. Builders have had to get creative or face steep fees for second utility hookups, second kitchens, and visible second entrances.[25] They're finding ways to work around these restrictions by creating, for example, kitchenettes instead of kitchens, concealing second front doors, and generally walking up to—but not actually crossing—the line between homes and duplexes, which have their own governmental rules and regulations.

Figuring Out the Finances

Multigenerational homes can offer many of the universal design features (e.g., main-floor bedroom suites and wider hallways) that facilitate aging in place. And code restrictions are starting to ease in certain jurisdictions as the demand for multigenerational housing grows.

But fully outfitted homes like the ones developed by Lennar's Next Gen, Toll Brothers, and CalAtlantic, for example, are on the pricier side, costing at least one-third more than conventional homes, which eliminates them as options for a lot of people. Next Gen's orchard model at Bulle Rock, for example, starts at $420,990 for 2,742 square feet, including a five-hundred-square-foot privacy suite.[26] By contrast, according to the US Census Bureau, the median sales price for a traditional single-family home in 2018 was $302,100.[27]

For mortgage purposes, multigens are financed as single-family homes. Typically, the senior parent makes the down payment, and the adult children are responsible for the loan. But, depending on your family's circumstance, other arrangements could also work.

Most of us don't have enough money for a down payment just lying around. For this to work, at least one participating adult would have to own a home and have equity that he or she didn't need to count as income to live on. This person would need to be willing to sell his or her existing residence(s) and to use the proceeds to pay down the cost of the multigen home to a level where the mortgage became affordable. And since there's typically only one name on a bank loan, that person would have to have the credit score to pull it off. True, these are steep requirements, but some families can meet them.

Multigenerational ADUs

ADU-type structures are designed to be built behind primary homes and are a much more affordable option that can meet a range of multigenerational needs. For example, as a way to downsize, earn incomes, and take care of extended families, some boomers are building ADU-type structures in their backyards. They then move out of their primary residences and into the ADUs and rent the big house to family members or tenants as a way to generate additional income.

For boomers who have this option or some variation of it, the affordability and income-generating potential of these ADUs can ease fears about not having enough to live on in the later years—or about running out of money altogether.

Rules for building ADUs vary by location, and you should study them very carefully before embarking on a building project. Check out Accessory Dwellings (https://accessorydwellings.org/adu-regulations

-by-city) for information on what rules may pertain to your area and to stay on top of developments in the ADU/multigen housing world.

You may also want to check out architect Deborah Pierce's book *The Accessible Home: Designing for All Ages and Abilities*, which covers hundreds of architectural and design ideas for life-span living. Now, some readers have complained that these ideas don't come cheap. Again, you don't have to take the whole bouquet. Check the book out from the library and see what can be plucked from it and adapted to your situation. What I like about Pierce's definition of *accessible* is that it moves beyond tacked-on grab bars. For her, *accessible* can be beautiful and functional.

Note to Builders and Developers

In addition to multigenerational houses for families, we need group housing suitable for mature adults. There's no need to get carried away. Skip the heated bathroom floors and wine cellars. Make them *affordable* and *sustainable*. Build in universal design features. The bedrooms should be of similar sizes and can be small—tiny, even— with functional bathrooms, but $1,700 (a price I have seen quoted in the Washington, DC, market) for a micro-bedroom adjacent to a common living area and kitchen is not affordable. Get creative with storage and shelving. Include lots of natural light and nooks and crannies where we can sit with our laptops and coffee. Intergenerational is a plus. And please don't build them too far out in "nowhere land"— at least not all of them, anyway! Walkability matters to a lot of us, as does easy access to public transportation and other basic amenities.

And dare I mention dormitories? We can't look at the near-poverty-level incomes of millions of boomers and not know that dormitories are on the horizon. So developers/builders/nonprofit housing advocates, why not get ahead of the curve with some innovation and interesting designs and financing options? Nobody wants to be warehoused in soulless concrete blocks of sameness. So, what's possible? If we don't start exploring this option now, we won't have to wait for the media's accounts of older adults living under appalling conditions. We'll already know about those conditions, because some of us will be among the ones living in them, along with our friends and family members.

Westminster Arcade, a former shopping mall in Providence, Rhode Island, was repurposed into "affordable" micro-apartments. True, it's not a dormitory, but it's the kind of out-of-the-grid thinking that we need: http://www.countryliving.com/real-estate/a35148 /shopping-mall-micro-homes-in-rhode-island.

Closer to the mark is the Commonspace Project in Syracuse, New York, which is dormitory living for adults (http://www.common space.io). Residents live in 300-square-foot micro-apartments built around a shared community space for cooking and gathering. The online brochure describes Commonspace as "taking the best parts of dorm living, community involvement, social interaction and applying them to downtown apartment living." Commonspace residents also have access to Syracuse CoWorks, a world-class coworking space and entrepreneurial hub. So, if you're a contract worker in the gig economy, you can move seamlessly between living and work. (I know, not everybody wants that!) Right now Commonspace targets millennials, but with some adaptation it could easily work for older adults too. True, many boomers on fixed incomes will find it pricey, with starting rents at $850 per month, but conceptually this kind of living and work space is moving in the right direction.

Others are jumping onto the shared housing, micro-apartment bandwagon like Common (https://www.common.com), with projects in Brooklyn, San Francisco, and Washington, DC, offering fully furnished private bedrooms, stocked kitchens, cleaning services, and on-the-premises washer and dryers. And WeWork has launched its own fully furnished collaborative habituation space, WeLive, with rents starting at about $1,640 per month, but rising steeply depending on the city.[28] Again, these developers are targeting millennials with over-the-top rents. Still, in terms of concept, we're in the right ballpark.

And because good ideas can come from anywhere, please check out Babayaga urban cohousing (http://seniorplanet.org/senior-housing -alternatives-urban-cohousing-the-babayaga-way), located in a Paris suburb and created by a group of older women committed to living independently into old age. One interesting feature about this project is that the cohousing collective secured nearly $4.4 million from eight government agencies to construct the building.

Following Your Interests to Friendship

Remember to do the "Top This" exercise and have three minutes of silence.

Many of us don't admit how alone and isolated we feel, and we can't begin to address that which we can't even admit is happening. Loneliness and social isolation are a national epidemic. Millions of Americans have landed here and not just people our age, but young adults, too.

Maintaining friendships takes work. I've found staying that involved and connected is a huge investment in time and attention. And let's face it, at our age, folks can get on your last nerve. But I find it affirming to have someone(s) to compare life notes with over a meal or coffee. It's validating to be seen and heard. But much more important than any of that, we know that staying connected with others is vitally important to our health and well-being. Social isolation can literally kill us.

◆ What does friendship mean to you? Must your friends share your same belief system, religion, political views? Or is it OK to have different core beliefs as long as you have shared hobbies and interests? My best friend is religious in a way I am not. That difference has not hampered our forty-year relationship. But it might be a difference that matters to you.

◆ Do your friends have to be your age? Every few months I get together with a group of young feminists thirty years my junior. I enjoy hearing about what's on their minds. I like interacting with people who are not all my age. They are more friendly acquaintances than friends.

◆ How much risk are you prepared to take to enlarge your friendship circles? There are certain risks in introducing yourself to a stranger, to inviting them to meet you for coffee at a café. I met the young women's group I mentioned earlier at my favorite neighborhood coffee shop. I was eavesdropping on their discussion, got to talking with them, and was invited to come to their next gathering. If I had been holed up at home, that opportunity would have never presented itself.

Are you willing to move outside your comfort zone to meet someone you might enjoy getting to know?

• I have found one of the best ways to make friends is to participate in an activity that requires you to meet with a group of people on a regular basis. Years ago, I was part of a group that volunteered to mentor some children. Before being assigned a child, we were required to complete training. Attending those training sessions was a natural way to get to know each other. We talked during the breaks and after class. Bonds developed over several weeks of training together. A number of friendships grew out of that experience. What free programs might you join? What group activities might you participate in? Think in terms of following your interests to friendship. Having interests in common (gardening, tennis, knitting, poetry . . . anything really) is a good basis on which to build friendship. Seeing the same people week after week gives you a chance to get to know them, and build trust. Real friendships can blossom from that fertile ground.

• And if all of this sounds like too much work, there are online sites like Stitch (https://www.stitch.net), a companionship, activities, and travel community for people over fifty. People do date, but it's not primarily a dating site. Its focus is on finding like-minded people to do things with. Stitch is a good option if you feel rusty socially and want guardrails before you get out there. It's hard to make connections, especially as we get older. It can be slow going. Stitch increases the number of people you can potentially meet, upping the possibility that you will find a group of people you like and want to get to know. Think of it as another tool in your kit.

Chapter 12

Strategic Responses to Housing

Wouldn't it be nice if there were tiny-home communities that
we empty-nesters in the fifty- to seventy-year-old age range who
are not yet ready for senior assisted living could downsize into?

—Liz

Tiny Houses: Downsizing without Downgrading

Tiny houses are not something people feel neutral about. The response is either "Are you kidding me?" or "Yeah, I could do that." In fact, in one recent survey, 57 percent of those over fifty-five gave living in a tiny home a thumbs-down.[1] Only 15 percent said they would definitely or seriously consider it. So it may come as a surprise that 40 percent of current tiny-home owners are over fifty years old.

But when you think about it, it makes sense. While these homes aren't cheap, some of the less expensive models are at least within reach for many boomers. Buying one is not a total impossibility. And financing options are getting better. Many of us want to downsize and be off the grid, and these small homes are less expensive to live in and relatively easy to maintain.

Tiny homes run the gamut from $2,000 shed-like structures like those built to house the homeless in Seattle[2] to tiny luxury abodes that cost hundreds of thousands of dollars.[3] Designing a tiny home that's too posh, though, defeats the point. Most people are moving into these tiny, affordable homes because they want to embrace simpler, less consumption-oriented lives.

The average tiny home is just under two hundred square feet, but "typical" homes can range from one hundred to four hundred square feet and can be built on foundations or on wheels. The point of demarcation, though, is not entirely clear to me, as I've seen many seven- and eight-hundred-square-foot homes claim the "tiny" label, and I've seen homes the size of my upstairs linen closet claim it too.

The average price of the standard 186-square-foot tiny home is $23,000 if you build it yourself, according to TinyLife.com. But it's not unusual for midrange homes to cost upward of $40,000. A custom-built house will typically run you $50,000 to $80,000 or more. But that's a far cry from the $302,100 median price tag for a traditional single-family house in the United States today.

And this affordability has caught the attention of many boomers, especially those on fixed incomes. These houses offer them chances to "small up" and to reduce housing costs to manageable levels, and some people pay off their tiny-home mortgages entirely. In fact, according to TinyHomes.com, 68 percent of those who own tiny homes don't have mortgages.

Getting Approval to Build a Tiny House

The tiny-house movement is a relatively recent phenomenon. In the world of zoning codes and ordinances, tiny houses are considered to be some newfangled thing—if they're even considered at all—and most municipalities have regulations that make it hard for home-owners to get approval to build or rent them. Pasadena, California, for example, "requires 15,000-square-foot lots to build them. Other cities require additional covered parking spots for each unit and utility hookup fees that cost tens of thousands of dollars."[4]

So while prospective owners may apply for and receive exemptions in some jurisdictions, they're likely looking at some very steep fees. That's why so many tiny houses are located in unincorporated areas and rural communities.

As the demand for ADUs/tiny houses has grown, state and municipal legislators have begun to ease restrictions. But they're not moving fast enough, given the growing demand for affordable housing in major urban markets where home prices are out of reach.

There are some hopeful signs. Cities like Santa Cruz and Portland, Oregon, for example, have updated ordinances and loosened municipal zoning regulations to support the proactive development of ADUs/tiny houses. But in general the rules are all over the map. So, if a tiny house is something that you'd really like to explore, it's imperative that you look at the rules for your area before building one. Check out the American Tiny House Association's website (http://american tinyhouseassociation.org/state-regulations) and "Cracking the Code: A Guide for Building Codes and Zoning for Tiny Houses" (http:// thetinylife.com/cracking-the-code-tiny-houses-and-building-codes).

Building a Tiny House

Lots of people save money by building their own tiny houses, and the Internet is full of online resources, how-to-get-started guides, lists of weekend seminars, customizable floor plans, and DIY shells to help with that. If you think you might want to take this route, you can check out the following: Niche (http://www.nichedesignbuild .com/about); PAD (https://padtinyhouses.com/the-big-idea); The Tiny House (http://www.thetinyhouse.net); The Tiny Project (http:// tiny-project.com/resources); Tiny House Build (https://tinyhouse build.com); and Relax Shacks (http://relaxshacks.blogspot.com).

Purchasing a Tiny House

If you're not the DIY type, you can purchase your tiny home. More and more builders are catering to the boomer market with universally designed spaces. Let's face it: at fifty-five or older, most of us won't be happy hoisting ourselves up narrow ladders to our loft beds to lie down with our faces four inches from the ceiling.

Check out these tiny-house builders who make single-floor models with bedroom suites on the main floors and steps instead of ladders: Brevard Tiny Homes (https://brevardtinyhouse.com); Fabcab (http://fabcab.com/about/our-story-and-bios); Humble Homes (http://humble-homes.com); Seattle Tiny Homes (http://seattle tinyhomes.com/models/#magnolia); Tiny Home Builders (https://www.tinyhomebuilders.com/tiny-houses/tiny-retirement#.VXm _sVxVikp); and Tumbleweed (http://www.tumbleweedhouses.com /pages/customize-your-tumbleweed?avad=141345_fc5e57bb).

And if you're selling the family home and have a few coins, you may want to check out companies like Tiny Heirloom, which can design pretty much whatever you want: https://www.tinyheirloom.com/3.

There are also so-called granny pods designed not only to support us as we age but also to help our parents and other loved ones we're assisting now. These ADUs/mobile units sit on the caregiver's property and go for between $85,000 and $125,000. I know: I had sticker shock too. But think of it this way: that's much less than the $40,000 or more per year that you'd have to shell out for an assisted-living facility. Obviously, this won't work for everybody, but what we need are options—multiple solutions—and this is one.

For granny pods, check out companies like Home Care Suites (http://www.homecaresuites.com); Next Door Housing (http://www .nextdoorhousing.com); and Elder Cottages (http://www.eldercottages .com/pricing.php).

And there are high-tech alternatives to nursing care like MedCottage (http://www.medcottage.com), which utilizes smart devices like medication dispensers, toilets that measure the volume of urine and its contents, and internet portals that monitor occupants' vital signs.

Financing a Tiny House

Financing options are available through some tiny-house manufacturers, like American Tiny House (https://www.americantinyhouse .com/ath-financing).

Tumbleweed (https://www.tumbleweedhouses.com/tiny-house-ru
-loans) is the only tiny house manufacturer I found to offer direct
financing.

If you have good to excellent credit, LightStream a division of
SunTrust Bank, can provided financing for your tiny home (https://
www.lightstream.com/tiny-houses).

Alex Pino of Tiny House Talks has put together a free fourteen-
page e-book on how to fund your tiny house. You can find it at
https://s3.amazonaws.com/tinyhousetalk/tiny-house-loans.pdf.

Chances are good that you won't be able to secure a regular mortgage for a tiny house on a foundation. There are building codes and
size requirements that it likely won't meet. Many buyers are able to
qualify for RV loans for their tiny houses on wheels, especially if their
builders have been designated as RV manufacturers, as, for example,
Tumbleweed has been. Check out Rock Solid Funding (https://www
.financemytrailer.com), which finances "non-motorized RVs."

Here's a final note: as the tiny-house movement gains national
momentum and zoning restrictions ease, we'll likely see an explo-
sion of tiny-house communities (like these: https://www.thespruce
.com/livable-tiny-house-communities-3984833) in response to the
lack of affordable housing. That will be a welcome development for
boomers on modest fixed incomes. Tiny houses have come a long
way since their rustic early days and offer affordable ways for older
adults to live in dignity and relative comfort. As lending institutions
catch up with the trend, more financing options should become
available. In the meantime, rent-to-buy programs can give residents
opportunities to build up equity over time. Again, there is no one
solution. Tiny houses are just one of many options we can consider.

I also want to give kudos to a tiny house that I just love. I have a
lot of African art from my travels and could really see myself living
here. Take a tour of Ms. Gypsy Soul's house here: http://msgypsy
soul.com/video-2. I've looked at hundreds of tiny houses now, and
there really is something for every budget and lifestyle preference.

Cohousing

I attended the Cohousing Association of America's annual conference in Durham, North Carolina, to learn more about shared-living models. Boomer interest in cohousing is on the rise. Growing numbers of us are looking for age-friendly, affordable housing options as an alternative to traditional retirement communities. We all remember visiting that elderly relative stuck in some drab, homogenized building with fluorescent lighting, weird hospital smells, and institutionalized food. We definitely don't want that for ourselves.

A majority of us wants to age in place, but not necessarily in the place we're living in right now. Economics will force some of us to move, and others will move by choice. Our traditional-style homes may have been fine when we didn't mind driving everywhere and maintenance wasn't such a chore and an expense, but many of us don't want that for ourselves now. We're weighing our housing options, including cohousing.

At the conference, boomers told me they liked cohousing's smaller living spaces and walkable design. They liked not having to depend on their cars to get around and did not miss lives built around highways. They said they welcomed feeling part of a community and big extended family, and that living in proximity with their neighbors curbed feelings of loneliness and isolation.

We boomers want to avoid institutional care and to live independently for as long as possible. Cohousing, with its built-in support networks, co-caring (within agreed-upon boundaries), and mutual assistance can help us to live how we want, knowing that neighbors are close by in case of an emergency or for the occasional helping hand.

Common Characteristics of Cohousing

The concept of cohousing was introduced into North America from Denmark in 1988 by American architects Charles Durrett and

Kathryn McCamant in their groundbreaking work *Cohousing: A Contemporary Approach to Housing Ourselves*. Durrett and Mc-Camant are also credited with designing Muir Commons (http://www.muircommons.org) in Davis, California, the first newly constructed cohousing community in the US, completed in 1991 and now celebrating its twenty-seventh year.

Today, over 165 cohousing communities have been built in twenty-five states and the District of Columbia, and more than 140 are currently under development.[5] Each cohousing community is uniquely planned and developed and can vary significantly in size, design, ownership structure, location, amenities, and purpose, but all share some defining characteristics. Mid Atlantic Cohousing[6] has developed a comprehensive list of common elements, and by pulling from this resource and others I have focused on five of the main ones below:

Resident Management: Residents organize and actively participate in the design and planning of the community from the ground up and are responsible for its ongoing management and maintenance.

Participatory Process: Residents have an active voice in community business and major decisions are made by consensus.

Intentional Site Design: The physical layout and orientation of the buildings aims to promote interaction between residents. Fully equipped single family homes, town houses, and rental units are arranged facing each other around common facilities with walkable and pedestrian friendly areas, and parking relegated to the periphery.

Common Facilities: Private living spaces have all of the amenities of traditional homes, but residents also have access to common facilities, which vary based on the needs of the community. Shared spaces include a common house, which typically has a community kitchen and large dining room for common meals and may include a lounge; a children's space; meeting rooms; an area for laundry; facilities for games, hobbies, and other recreational activities; and guest rooms for family and friends. Outdoor shared spaces/resources may include flower and vegetable gardens, playgrounds, basketball courts, lawn care and snow removal equipment, toolsheds, and the like.

Shared Values: More than architecture, cohousing is a way of living, sharing, and relying on one another in resident-created neighborhoods. It supports consciously living in community through sharing tasks, activities, and decision-making.

For a curated list of additional resources on cohousing, please see http://www.midatlanticcohousing.org/uploads/5/7/9/8/57982291 /some_cohousing_resouces_19.pdf and also http://www.cohousing .org.

Diversity of Expression

One of the things I have noticed after viewing dozens of photos of cohousing communities is that at this point there appear to be very few people of color. I noticed this, too, at the cohousing conference I attended, where I was one of about six people of color among approximately 450 attendees.

Cohousing advocates and critics alike have also noticed that the movement tends to attract mainly white, educated, middle- and upper-middle-income people. Why does this matter? you ask. Because the very people who could well benefit the most from cohousing's sharing and mutual support model—low- and moderate-income families, working single mothers, and vulnerable seniors—are priced out of most communities.

That said, cohousing advocates and developers are aware of these challenges and are adapting the traditional cohousing model, adding more affordable units, figuring out how to better incorporate the needs of seniors, opening up to renters, becoming more intentional about inclusion, and exploring how to use the skills and talents of cohousing residents to tackle problems in our society at large.

In a very thoughtful article on cohousing and ethnic and racial diversity, Zev Paiss, director of project development for Support Financial Services, and former founding executive director of the Cohousing Network, talks candidly about the issues and offers some thoughts on a way forward. You can read it here: http://www.ic.org /wiki/desire-diversity-cohousing-perspective.

The People of Color Sustainable Housing Network was founded in February 2015 as a meet-up group "hosting events, trainings and field visits to cohousing, cooperative and farm sites led and owned by people of color in the Bay Area." The POCSHN is a resource guide for people of color "committed to creating an entire ecosystem of POC-centered cohousing, cooperative housing and intentional communities that are ecologically, emotionally, spiritually, and culturally regenerative spaces." You can learn more about POCSHN at http://www.pochousingnetwork.com.

Affordability

Cohousing has the reputation for being pricey and out of reach for most people. Use of green design and construction methods comes at a cost. And added to it is the prorata share of the common facilities that each future cohousing owner must pay. But sustainable construction delivers major economic benefits too in ongoing cost savings on operations, maintenance and utilities. So, when assessing cohousing affordability, the upfront costs *and* long-term savings have to be taken into account—and not just savings on operating costs but savings on shared meals, child care, transportation, equipment, tools, and the like that add up.

While most cohousing communities are made up of market priced homes, some have incorporated affordable housing.[7] At Silver Sage Village in Boulder, Colorado, for example, six of the sixteen homes are designated as permanently affordable by the Boulder Housing Authority (http://silversagevillage.com).

Petaluma Avenue Homes (http://www.sahahomes.org/properties /petaluma-avenue-homes), located in Sebatopol, California, is one of the first entirely affordable rental cohousing communities in the country. Completed in 2009 by nonprofit developer Affordable Housing Associates, Petaluma serves low-income families and seniors making 30 to 50 percent of area mean income. The community comprises forty-five apartments and town houses with cohousing design and social principles applied to the common house, community garden, and open areas.

The government has a role to play if we want to realize fully the potential of cohousing as a residential solution for low and moderate income households, including seniors. The twenty-nine-unit Elder Spirit Community (http://www.elderspirit.org) at Trailview in Abingdon, Virginia, is an example of what public-private partnerships can achieve. Elder Spirit is "an intentional mixed-income cohousing community of elders (55+) committed to growing old with spirit, recognizing that this time of our lives is the time to explore and cultivate the spiritual aspects of our nature."

It is the first mixed income cohousing community for seniors that includes both private ownership and rental properties. The $3.6 million development was financed by a combination of public grants, private donations, and loans, which included support from the Virginia Housing Development Authority, the Virginia Department of Housing and Community Development, and the Federal Home Loan Bank.[8] Elder Spirit has thirteen market rate and sixteen affordable units with rents from $373 to $535 for one- and two-bedroom apartments. As these apartments are constructed with government funding, prospective tenants much meet strict income eligibility requirements.

Focused advocacy is also critical. Partnerships for Affordable Cohousing (http://www.affordablecohousing.org) is a nonprofit committed to "partnerships between cohousing and affordable housing advocates to further affordable cohousing in mixed income cohousing communities." PFAC also provides technical assistance to existing cohousing groups and groups in formation that are committed to integrating low- and moderate-income households into their communities.

The bottom line is that we have residential solutions that can help people who need low-cost housing. It's not like we have nothing that can be scaled. What we don't have is supportive legislation for cohousing, for tiny houses, and for multigen homes. Builders and developers have to get creative to navigate their way around zoning and building codes written for another era.

Here is a case that is illustrative: All Alice Green, seventy-two, wanted was to get a reverse mortgage on her cohousing condominium in Berkley, California, just like tens of thousands of other seniors. But HUD regional staff declined her application. According to Alice, "Anyone else in my situation could apply for a reverse mortgage. But somehow because my neighbors and I share some meals and resources like a laundry room, the Federal Housing Administration (FHA) won't treat us the same as other condominium communities and won't allow even a small reverse mortgage for my home."[9]

It took over two years and a "Help Alice Save Her Home" petition signed by over 10,000 people for the US Department of Housing and Urban Development (HUD), to change policy and "treat cohousing condominiums the same as other condominiums for the purpose of certifying a cohousing project for federally backed mortgage insurance."[10]

Financiers, too, are finding that their hands are tied. Some tiny houses, for example, masquerade as RVs so their buyers can qualify for loans. Given the magnitude of the affordable housing shortage, you'd think we could do better than this piecemeal approach. We understand that zoning and building codes are for our own protection. No issue there: we want to live in safe well-built structures. But safety need not be incompatible with housing innovation and new ways of doing things.

As a country, we have achieved longevity by investing tens of billions of dollars in the diagnosis, management, and treatment of disease. And it has paid off. Tens of millions of us will live well into our seventies and eighties. But where and under what circumstances?

We have prolonged our existence, but have not been as successful investing in the *physical infrastructure* needed to support our health, emotional well-being, dignity, and independence as we age.

That's what we've got to do now. And we're playing catch-up. Big-time.

Resilience Circle Reflection

Smalling Up

Remember to do the "Top This" exercise and to have three minutes of silence.

You have choices about where and how you live. Only you know what you truly can afford. Even on a modest budget you have options. Now is a good time to figure out where you ultimately want to land. Does cohousing's emphasis on community, lifelong learning, and participatory process appeal to you? Or maybe you qualify for a reverse mortgage, or can picture yourself in a tiny house, an adult dormitory, or sharing your current residence with a group of friends. Or maybe you want to flip the script totally and become part of the expatriate community in San Miguel de Allende or some other place that allows you to live on a tiny fraction of what it costs you to live in the US. Now is the time to begin exploring what is possible.

◆ When you read about the various residential options, is there one that fits your situation better than the others? And if you don't like any of the options available to you, is one, at least, less objectionable than the others? If you're in a situation where you're going to have to move, maybe you start your exploration there.

◆ Let's say circumstances are such that you do have to move from a place you have lived for decades. You simply cannot afford to live there anymore. You feel devastated and adrift. You can't imagine living anywhere else. How do you deal with the roller coaster of emotions you're feeling? Anyone who has stood in these shoes, please share your experience. Talk about how you coped and how you clawed your way back, how you reconciled yourself to the choices you had to make.

◆ Are you eligible for government subsidized housing? If you're sixty-two or older and have limited income you may qualify for affordable senior housing under HUD's Section 202 program, http://www.need helppayingbills.com/html/section_202_housing.html. Have you applied? Yeah, we know how long the wait can be. But here's the thing: you can't even be considered if you're not on the list, however long it is. So, please, get on the list. Live your life while you wait. Keep it moving. If you're called, consider it a blessing.

◆ Are you eligible for a reverse mortgage? Find out here: https://www .ncoa.org/economic-security/home-equity/housing-options/use -your-home-to-stay-at-home. The point is to look at all of our options and leave no stone unturned.

◆ Would you consider taking on a housemate to cut your expenses? Are there any changes you would need to make to your home before another person could reside there? Chapter 11 includes free and low-cost resources for making minor home repairs to support aging in place. Do you meet any of the program eligibility requirements?

◆ Depending on your habits, getting rid of decades of accumulated stuff can be a straight vertical lift. Are you ready to trudge up that hill? What change in your attitude about this task could make it easier? Is there a friend who can help you or a group of friends who can help each other?

You have now finished the last chapter in *55, Underemployed, and Faking Normal.* I suggest you meet once more to celebrate/honor your time together and the work you've done. It's also an opportunity to decide whether you wish to continue on as a group or disband. And you may have a situation where some wish to continue and others feel your group's work together is complete. Each group will be different and there's no right or wrong path. Those who wish to continue on may wish to meet at another time and figure out what the next steps look like for them.

Conclusion

I wish we had met, that I could speak with each one of you, and know your story, and tell you more about my own.

I hope this book has been a support to you and that you have found community in your Resilience Circle and beyond, and resources to illuminate your path.

If this has been a particularly hard time for you, I hope that you have found some measure of solace in the words of your contemporaries. I know that the facts of your particular circumstance may not have changed. You may still not be working or not have the income you need. But it counts if how you're holding these things has shifted, if you've managed to loosen the grip of the negative self-talk and failure label that was drowning you before. Progress starts with that first step.

My hope is that after reading this book:

- You know that you're not alone, not by a long shot. There is strength in numbers and we can use smart technology to stay connected and learn from one another.

- You realize that there is no one right way forward. We're in the middle of a massive paradigm shift. Much of what we know has been turned on its head. We're going to make mistakes. Learn from them. Forgive yourself. Focus on what is working. Throw away the rest.

- You're faking normal less or not at all. You've had the conversations with the people who need to know the details of what you're going through. You're declining the invitations you can't afford and are being candid with friends and family.

- You're getting the help you need and see it as strategy not failure.

- You're taking better care of your body and being kinder to yourself.

- You've developed more clarity around what you need to feel grounded and content in this next phase of life. You're putting into action what you've learned and taking the opportunity of this economic crisis to come out better.

- You see possibility where you saw none before and are moving through the world a more curious person, willing to consider options you would have rejected outright before.

- Your own entrepreneurial mind-set has been activated and you're coming up with ideas and projects that you could launch on your own or with others, small or big: it doesn't matter.

And, finally, I want to hear from you. Let me know how you're doing and where you think we can go from here. You can reach me by email on lizzy@55andfakingnormal.com, on my website (http://55andfakingnormal.com), or follow me on Twitter @55and fakingnormal.

—Elizabeth

Acknowledgments

You don't write a book alone. I really lucked out by getting a mom like Dotte White. It just doesn't get better. *Fierce* is how I would describe her unwavering support. Thank you.

I also thank my daughter, Rhonda, who has walked with me every step of the way. It has been a great comfort during this stressful period watching her put into action what she knows, and what I taught her, blossoming into the amazing young woman she's become.

And I thank my grandson, George, who kept his Nana laughing and focused on what's important in life.

I thank my brother Chris for giving me the idea to write this book and for our many discussions about it.

I thank Richard Eisenberg from *Next Avenue*, who took a chance on me, an unknown author, and published "You Know Her," my first essay on aging. I thank the thousands of you who commented and "liked" the essay on PBS's FB page, and the hundreds who took the time to write to me directly to share your personal stories. I am grateful. You've taught me so much. This book would not have been possible without you.

I owe profound thanks to Paul Solmon from PBS NewsHour's Making Sen$e for seeing the value of my work early on and inviting me to share my story on air and reach a much larger audience than I could have on my own.

My gratitude to Bob Bender for his keen editorial eye, skill, and sensitivity in helping me to build on my earlier work and make it better.

I thank Juanita Briton, Joyce Ballard, Sharon Freeman, and Elijah for believing in this work from the beginning and helping me to keep it going when things looked dicey.

ACKNOWLEDGMENTS

I thank Dine Watson, fellow author and friend, for the scaffolding she provided throughout my writing process, for validating my voice and vision, and for being there for me through life's ups and downs.

I thank my best friend, Florie Liser, for her very helpful editing suggestions, for being a steadfast believer in this project, and for encouraging me as it unfolded.

I thank Joia Nuri for telling her truth and hearing mine, for being there for me through the beautiful and the unbeautiful. It has made all the difference.

I thank Taquiena Boston, a literal font of information and resources, for our many discussions about the book and her thoughtful suggestions about ways to improve it.

I owe grateful thanks to Deborah Burkholder for her rolled-up-sleeves involvement and review and critique of the entire manuscript. I thank her, too, for introducing me to her colleagues at the Institute for Career Transitions and for inviting me to speak at ICT's biannual conference not once but twice.

Many thanks to Nicole Miles for designing the original edition of the website, and for always going above and beyond on all that I asked of her.

I acknowledge with much appreciation Pamela Ferrell, who insisted that the book be solutions oriented and link readers to useful resources.

I thank my dear friend Julius Ware II for believing in me always, for cheering me on, and for being the first person to buy my book.

I offer heartfelt thanks to those who reviewed all or part of the manuscript offering their insight, feedback, and words of encouragement: Pamela Anderson, Marquette Folley, Nahuja Maddox, Tom McDonough, Michelle Owens, Scott Schulz, Denise Washington, and my sister, Alyssa White.

I thank my friend Jeff Majors for listening to me read aloud from the manuscript, affirming the work I was doing, and telling me early and often, "I know a hit when I hear one."

Notes

Chapter 1: Lost, Ashamed, and Shell-shocked

1. "How Much Should I Save Each Year?" Fidelity Viewpoints, June 5, 2017, https://www.fidelity.com/viewpoints/retirement/how-much-money-should-I-save.

2. Ben Steverman, "Two-thirds of Americans Aren't Putting Money in Their 401(k)," Bloomberg, February 21, 2017, https://www.bloomberg.com/news/articles/2017-02-21/two-thirds-of-americans-aren-t-putting-money-in-their-401-k.

3. "Backgrounder: What is the Retirement?" The New School SCEPA, February 22, 2018, http://www.economicpolicyresearch.org/retirement-tools/the-retirement-crisis.

4. AARP, 2016 Longevity Economy Snapshot Infographic, file:///C:/Users/CGF/AppData/Local/Temp/2016-Longevity-Economy-Snapshot-Infographic-AARP.pdf.

5. Alicia H. Munnell and We Liang Hou, "Will Millennials Be Ready for Retirement?" Center for Retirement Research at Boston College, January 2018, crr.bc.edu/wp-content/uploads/2018/01/1B_18-2.pdf.

6. Alana Semuels, "This Is What Life Without Retirement Savings Looks Like," *Atlantic*, February 22, 2018, https://www.theatlantic.com/business/archive/2018/02/pensions-safety-net-california/553970/8.

7. The third nut, of course, is health care . . . It's huge, I know, but it's beyond the scope of this particular project.

Chapter 3: Shock and Awe

1. Jack VanDerhei, Ph.D., "Bridging the Gap: How Prepared are Americans for Retirement?" United States Senate Special Committee on Aging, March 12, 2015, https://www.ebri.org/pdf/publications/testimony/T-182.pdf.
2. YiLi Chien, Paul Morris, "Many Americans Still Lack Retirement Savings," Federal Reserve Bank of St. Louis, First Quarter 2018, https://www.stlouis fed.org/publications/regional-economist/first-quarter-2018/many-ameri cans-still-lack-retirement-savings.
3. *Report on the Economic Well-Being of U.S. Households in 2017*, Board of Governors of the Federal Reserve System, May 2018, https://www.federal reserve.gov/publications/files/2017-report-economic-well-being-us-house holds-201805.pdf.
4. Heather Gillers, Ann Tergesen and Leslie Scism, "A Generation of Americans is Entering Old Age the Least Prepared in Decades," *Wall Street Journal*, June 22, 2018, https://www.wsj.com/articles/a-generation-of -americans-is-entering-old-age-the-least-prepared-in-decades-1529676033.
5. "Measures of Central Tendency for Wage Data," Social Security, Office of the Chief Actuary, 2018, https://www.ssa.gov/oact/cola/central.html.
6. "Wage Statistics for 2016," Social Security, Office of the Chief Actuary, 2018, https://www.ssa.gov/cgi-bin/netcomp.cgi?year=2018.
7. "Federal Poverty Level," Healthcare.gov, 2018, https://www.healthcare.gov /glossary/federal-poverty-level-FPL/.
8. The United Way ALICE Project, Working Hard, But Struggling to Survive, United Way of Northern New Jersey, May 2018, https://www.united wayalice.org/home. The United Way ALICE Project is a collaboration of United Ways in Connecticut, Florida, Hawaii, Idaho, Louisiana, Maryland, Michigan, Ohio, Oregon, Pennsylvania, Texas, Virginia, Washington and Wisconsin.
9. McGrath, Maggie, "63% of Americans Don't Have Enough Savings to Cover a $500 Emergency," *Forbes*, January 6, 2016, https://www.forbes.com/sites /maggiemcgrath/2016/01/06/63-of-americans-dont-have-enough-savings -to-cover-a-500-emergency/#476e14094e0d.
10. Board of Governors of the Federal Reserve System, *Report on the Economic Well-Being of U.S. Households in 2017* (May 2018), https://www .federalreserve.gov/publications/files/2017-report-economic-well-being-us -households-201805.pdf.
11. Bureau of Labor Statistics, Economic News Release, "Household Data:

Alternative Measures of Labor Utilization," https://www.bls.gov/news .release/empsit.t15.htm.

12. Glossary of U.S. Bureau of Labor Statistics, https://www.bls.gov/bls /glossary.htm.

13. The New School SCEPA Jobs Report, "38% of 1.1 Million Jobless Older Workers Left Out of the Unemployment Rate are Poor," July 6, 2018, http://www.economicpolicyresearch.org/jobs-report/june-2018-unemploy ment-report-for-workers-over-55.

14. The New School SCEPA Jobs Report, "Unstable or Low-Wage Jobs Make Up More than 1/2 of Older Workers' Job Growth," May 4,2018, http:// www.economicpolicyresearch.org/jobs-report/april-2018-unemployment -report-for-workers-over-55

15. Teresa Ghilarducci, "Unprepared: Our Flawed Retirement System," Reflec- tions, Yale University, 2013, http://reflections.yale.edu/article/test-time-art -aging/unprepared-our-flawed-retirement-system.

16. "The Retirement Breach in Defined Contributions Plans," HelloWallet, 2013, file:///C:/Users/CGE/AppData/Local/Temp/HelloWallet_The%20Retire mentBreachInDefinedContributionPlans.pdf.

17. Helaine Olen, "Buying Coffee Every Day Isn't Why You're in Debt," Slate, May 26, 2016, http://www.slate.com/articles/business/the_united_states _of_debt/2016/05/the_latte_is_a_lie_and_buying_coffee_has_nothing_to _do_with_debt_an_excerpt.html.

18. Helaine Olen, "Giving Up Coffee to Balance the Books: How Many Lattes to Financial Freedom," Helaine's Blog, August 13, 2013, http://helaineolen .com/2013/08/13/giving-up-coffee-to-balance-the-books-how-many-lattes -to-financial-freedom/.

Chapter 4: After a Lifetime of Work, How Did We Land Here?

1. "Average Monthly Social Security Payment to Retired Female Workers in the U.S. from 2007 to 2017 (in U.S. dollars)," Statista, https://www.statista .com/statistics/194320/average-social-security-payment-made-to-retired -female-workers-monthly/.

2. "Average Monthly Social Security Payment to Retired Male Workers in the U.S. from 2007 to 2017 (in U.S. dollars)," Statista, https://www.statista .com/statistics/194313/average-social-security-payment-made-to-retired -male-workers-monthly/.

3. Juliette Cubanski, Kendal Orgera, Anthony Damico, and Tricia Neuman,

"How Many Seniors Are Living in Poverty? National and State Estimates Under the Official and Supplemental Poverty Measures in 2016," Henry J. Kaiser Family Foundation, March 2, 2018, https://www.kff.org/medicare/issue-brief/how-many-seniors-are-living-in-poverty-national-and-state-estimates-under-the-official-and-supplemental-poverty-measures-in-2016/.

4. Jill Schlesinger, "Half of U.S. Women Fear Becoming 'Bag Ladies,'" Moneywatch, CBS News.com, http://www.cbsnews.com/news/half-of-us-women-fear-becoming-bag-ladies/.

5. Index Mundi, "United States Demographic Profile 2018," January 20, 2018, https://www.indexmundi.com/united_states/demographics_profile.html.

6. Eric Morath, "Gender Wage Gap Narrows to Smallest on Record," *Wall Street Journal*, September 13, 2016. "Cornell researchers estimate that about half of the gap stems from women being more clustered in lower paying jobs and industries—not that they are paid less for identical work. Around one-sixth comes from men being on the job longer. Just over one-third of the gap comes from factors that can't be easily pinned down including potential discrimination."

7. Ariane Hegewisch, M. Phil, and Emma Williams-Baron, "The Gender Wage Gap: 2016 Earnings Differences by Gender, Race, and Ethnicity," Institute for Women's Policy Research, September 13, 2017, https://iwpr.org/publications/gender-wage-gap-2016-earnings-differences-gender-race-ethnicity/#_edn6.

8. "The Top Ten Facts About the Gender Wage Gap," Center for American Progress, April 12, 2016, https://www.americanprogress.org/issues/women/report/2016/04/12/135260/the-top-10-facts-about-the-gender-wage-gap/.

9. Family Caregiver Alliance, "Caregiver Statistics: Work and Caregiving," 2016, https://www.caregiver.org/caregiver-statistics-work-and-caregiving.

10. Jennifer Erin Brown, Nari Rhee, Joelle Saad-Lester, and Diane Oakley, *Shortchanged in Retirement* (Washington, DC: National Institute on Retirement Security, 2016), http://www.nirsonline.org/storage/nirs/documents/Shortchanged/final_shortchanged_retirement_report_2016.pdf.

11. Woman View, *Older Women and Poverty* (Sargent Shriver Center on Poverty and Law, 2016), http://www.ncdsv.org/SSNCPL_Woman-View-Older-Women-and-Poverty_3-30-2016.pdf.

12. Teresa Ghilarducci, Michael Papadopoulos, and Anthony Webb, "40 Percent of Older Workers and Their Spouses Will Experience Downward Mobility in Retirement," Schwartz Center for Economic Policy Analysis, February 2018, file:///C:/Users/CGE/AppData/Local/Temp/Downward_Mobility_in_Retirement_PN.pdf.

13. Alicia H. Munnell and Anqui Chen, "401(k)/IRA Holdings in 2016: An Update from the SCF," Center for Retirement Research at Boston College, October 2017, Number 17-18, file:///C:/Users/CGE/AppData/Local/Temp /IB_17-18.pdf.

14. Ilana Bovi and Nari Rhee, "The Continuing Retirement Savings Crisis," National Institute on Retirement Security, March 2015, https://www.nirson line.org/reports/the-continuing-retirement-savings-crisis/.

15. "The Assets & Opportunity Score Card," Corporation for Enterprise Development, 2016, http://assetsandopportunity.org/scorecard/.

16. ERISA Benefits Consulting, Inc., "401(K) Plan Participates Yawn over New Fee Disclosures," HG.org Legal Resources, https://www.hg.org/article .asp?id=30371.

17. Robert Reich, "Almost 80 Percent of US Workers Live from Paycheck to Paycheck. Here's why," *The Guardian*, July 29, 2018, https://www .theguardian.com/commentisfree/2018/jul/29/us-economy-workers-pay check-robert-reich.

18. US Census Bureau, Quarterly Residential Vacancies and Homeownership, First Quarter 2018, April 26, 2018, file:///C:/Users/CGE/AppData/Local /Temp/currenthvspress-1.pdf.

19. "The Road to Retirement," *New York Times*, Sunday Review, September 15, 2012, http://www.nytimes.com/2012/09/16/opinion/sunday/the-road -to-retirement.html?hp&_r=1.

20. "A Deeper Dive into Decreasing Home Values," Zillow Real Estate Analytics, September 2015.

21. Haas Institute for a Fair and Inclusive Society, *Underwater America: How the So-Called Housing "Recovery" Is Bypassing Most American Communities*, 2014, http://haasinstitute.berkeley.edu/sites/default/files/haasinstitute _underwateramerica_publish_0.pdf.

22. Zillow Group, "Finding Home as a Person of Color," Consumer Housing Trends Report 2017, https://www.zillow.com/report/2017/highlights/find ing-home-person-color/.

23. Biggs, Andrew, "How much do retirees really depend on social security?" AEI Economics, March 28, 2018, http://www.aei.org/publication/how-much-do -retirees-really-depend-on-social-security-far-less-than-youd-think/.

24. Transamerica Center for Retirement Studies, *The Retirement Readiness of Three Unique Generations: Baby Boomers, Generation X, and Millennials* (April 2014), https://www.transamericacenter.org/docs/default-source/re sources/center-research/tcrs2014_sr_three_unique_generations.pdf.

Chapter 5: Grabbing Denial by the Lapels

1. *How Do Families Cope with Financial Shocks: The Role of Emergency Savings in Family Financial Security*, Pew Charitable Trusts, October 2015, http://www.pewtrusts.org/~/media/assets/2015/10/emergency-savings-report-1_artfinal.pdf?la=en.
2. *The Precarious State of Family Balance Sheets*, Pew Charitable Trusts, January 2015, http://www.pewtrusts.org/~/media/assets/2015/01/fsm_balance_sheet_report.pdf.
3. Charles Babington, "Americans' Financial Security and Mobility: Key Factors," *Trust* magazine, Pew, July 28, 2017, http://magazine.pewtrusts.org/en/archive/summer-2017/americans-financial-security-and-mobility-key-factors.

Chapter 6: Smalling Up: Rethinking Limits, Lack, and Deprivation

1. Stephanie Land, "The Class Politics of Decluttering," *New York Times*, Opinion Page, July 18, 2016, http://www.nytimes.com/2016/07/18/opinion/the-class-politics-of-decluttering.html?_r=1.

Chapter 7: Circling the Drain

1. *Chronic Conditions Among Older Americans*, AARP, http://assets.aarp.org/rgcenter/health/beyond_50_hcr_conditions.pdf.
2. "SNAP: Requirements for Able-bodied Adults without Dependents," United States Department of Agriculture, Food and Nutrition Service, February 26, 2018, https://www.fns.usda.gov/snap/fr-022318.

Chapter 9: The Changing World of Work

1. David Gelles, The WeWork Manifesto: First, Office Space. Next, the World." *New York Times*, February 17, 2018, https://www.nytimes.com/2018/02/17/business/the-wework-manifesto-first-office-space-next-the-world.html.
2. Sara Horowitz, "Freelancing in America 2017," Freelancers Union, October 17, 2017, https://blog.freelancersunion.org/2017/10/17/freelancing-in-america-2017/.
3. Jonathan V. Hall and Alan B. Kruger, *An Analysis of the Labor Markets*

for Uber's Driver Partners in the United States, January 22, 2015, https://s3.amazonaws.com/uber-static/comms/PDF/Uber_Driver-Partners_Hall_Kreuger_2015.pdf.

4. *Airbnb's Growing Community of 60+ Women Hosts,* Airbnb, 2016, https://www.airbnbaction.com/wp-content/uploads/2016/03/Airbnb_60_Plus_Women_Report.pdf.

5. Jacob Bogage, "How Much Uber Drivers Actually Make per Hour," *Washington Post,* June 27, 2016, https://www.washingtonpost.com/news/the-switch/wp/2016/06/27/how-much-uber-drivers-actually-make-per-hour/#comments.

6. Robert Reich, "Why the Shared Economy Is Harming Workers and What Must be Done," Robert Reich (blog), November 27, 2015, http://robertreich.org/post/134080559175.

7. Meredith Carey, "Paris Could Pull 43,000 Airbnb Listings by This June," *Condé Nast Traveler,* April 12, 2018, https://www.cntraveler.com/story/paris-could-pull-43000-airbnb-listings-by-this-june.

8. Rupert Jones, "Airbnb wrecks travelers' holiday plans as battle with cities intensifies," *The Guardian,* June 16, 2018, https://www.theguardian.com/technology/2018/jun/16/airbnb-booking-cancelled-last-minute-holiday-wrecked#comments.

9. Fergus O'Sullivan, "Berlin Just Canceled It's Airbnb Ban," City Lab, March 23, 2018, https://www.citylab.com/life/2018/03/berlin-airbnb-vacation-rental-regulation-law/556397/.

10. Reuters Staff, "Uber loses EU court case in fight against French criminal charges," *Reuters,* April 10, 2018, https://www.reuters.com/article/us-uber-court-eu/uber-loses-eu-court-case-in-fight-against-french-criminal-charges-idUSKBN1HH0W4.

11. Henry Goldman, "Suicides, Traffic Hell in NYC Spur Second Look at Uber Growth," *Bloomberg,* June 18, 2018, https://www.bloomberg.com/news/articles/2018-06-18/suicides-traffic-hell-in-nyc-spur-second-look-at-uber-s-growth.

12. Robert W. Fairlie, Arnobia Morelix, E. J. Reedy, and Inara Tareque, *The 2017 Kaufman Index Startup Activity National Trends,* Kauffman Foundation, May 2017, https://www.kauffman.org/kauffman-index/reporting/startup-activity/~/media/c9831094536646528ab012dcbd1f83be.ashx.

13. Statistics about business size including small businesses, US Census Bureau.

14. Sangeeta Bharadwaj Bandal and Bryant Ott, "A Very Fast-Growing Group

of Entrepreneurs: People Over 50," Gallup, January 29, 2015, http://www
.gallup.com/businessjournal/181352/fast-growing-group-entrepreneurs
-people.aspx.

15. Jessica Stillman, "How to Double Your Chances of Founding a Successful Startup: Get a Couple of Decades Older," Inc.com, June 2018, https://
www.inc.com/jessica-stillman/how-to-double-your-chances-of-founding-a
-successful-startup-get-a-couple-of-decades-older.html.

16. Zoe Bernard, "The idea that most successful startup founders are in their
twenties is a myth—the average entrepreneur is much older," *Business
Insider*, April 24, 2018, http://markets.businessinsider.com/news/stocks
/young-startup-founder-myth-average-age-of-entrepreneurs-42-mit-study
-2018-4-1022156654.

17. Mark S. Granovetter, "The Strength of Weak Ties," *American Journal of
Sociology* 78, no. 6 (May 1973): 1360–80, https://sociology.stanford.edu
/sites/default/files/publications/the_strength_of_weak_ties_and_exch_w
-gans.pdf.

18. Lydia DePillis, "Baby Boomers Are Taking on Ageism and Losing," *Washington Post*, August 4, 2016, https://www.washingtonpost.com/lifestyle
/magazine/baby-boomers-are-taking-on-ageism—and-losing/2016/08/03
/43d6664c-120c-11e6-8967-7ac733c56f12_story.html?wpisrc=n1_most
&wpmm=1.

19. Jeff Cox, "U.S. Unemployed Have Quit Looking for Jobs at a 'Frightening'
Level: Survey," CNBC, June 8, 2016, http://www.cnbc.com/2016/06/08
/us-unemployed-have-quit-looking-for-jobs-at-a-frightening-level-survey
.html?_source=newsletter%7Ceven ingbrief.

Chapter 10: Thinking Outside the ~~Box~~ Country

1. "Cost of Living Halved for Expats in Mexico," *Mexico Daily News*, February 8, 2018, https://mexiconewsdaily.com/news/cost-of-living-halved-for
-expats-in-mexico/?utm_source=Mexico+News+Daily&utm_campaign
=2b7a2037d8-newsletter&utm_medium=email&utm_term=0
_f1536a3787-2b7a2037d8-34 9459241.

2. To get a *general* idea of the costs of living in San Miguel de Allende, check
out Expatistan, Cost of Living, San Miguel, 2018, https://www.expatistan
.com/cost-of-living/san-miguel-de-allende, and Nubeo, Cost of Living,
San Miguel, https://www.numbeo.com/cost-of-living/in/San-Miguel-de
-Allende.

Chapter 11: Retirement Security Requires Housing Security

1. AARP Public Policy Institute, *Sources of Income for Older Americans, 2012* (December 2013), http://www.aarp.org/content/dam/aarp/research/public _policy_institute/econ_sec/2013/sources-of-income-for-older-americans -20 12-fs-AARP-ppi-econ-sec.pdf.

2. *Retirement Security: Most Households Approaching Retirement Have Low Savings* (Washington, DC: US Government Accountability Office, 2015), http://www.gao.gov/assets/680/670153.pdf.

3. "Making America Unaffordable Again," RealtyTrac, June 30, 2017, https: //wpnewsroom.realtytrac.com/news/making-america-unaffordable -again/.

4. Andrew Woo, "How Have Rents Changed Since 1960," Apartment List .com, June 14, 2016, https://www.apartmentlist.com/rentonomics/rent -growth-since-1960/.

5. *Housing America's Older Adults: Meeting the Needs of an Aging Population*, Joint Center for Housing Studies of Harvard University, 2014, http:// www.jchs.harvard.edu/sites/default/files/jchs-housing_americas_older _adults_2014_0.pdf. A severe burden means spending half or more of the household income on housing; a moderate burden means spending 30 to 50 percent of the income on it.

6. Alan Kline, "Think of Affordable Housing as an Opportunity, Not an Obligation," *American Banker*, January 2016, http://www.americanbanker.com /news/national-regional/think-of-affordable-housing-as-an opportunity-not -an-obligation-1078541-1.html.

7. Andrew Aurand, Dan Emmanuel, Diane Yentel, Ellen Errico, Jared Gaby-Biegel, and Emma Kerr, *Out of Reach, the High Cost of Housing*, National Low Income Housing Coalition, 2018, http://nlihc.org/sites/default/files /oor/OOR_2018.pdf.

8. "The Cost of Affordable Housing: Does It Pencil Out?" Urban Institute, July 2016, http://apps.urban.org/features/cost-of-affordable-housing/.

9. Erika C. Poethig, "One in Four: America's Housing Assistance Lottery," Urban Wire, Urban Institute, May 28, 2014, http://www.urban.org/urban -wire/one-four-americas-housing-assistance-lottery.

10. Fin Lan and Susan L. Brown, "Unmarried Boomers Confront Old Age: A National Portrait," *Gerontologist* 52, no. 2 (April 2012): 153–65, http:// gerontologist.oxfordjournals.org/content/52/2/153.full.

11. Carol Marak, "Elder Orphans Have a Harder Time Aging in Place," Next Avenue, September 8, 2016, https://www.nextavenue.org/elder-orphans-harder-aging-place/.

12. Julianne Holt Lunstad, Timothy B. Smith, and Jay Bradley Layton, "Social Relationships and Mortality Risk: A Meta-analytic Review," *PLOS Medicine 7*, no. 7 (July 27, 2010), doi: 10.1371/journal, http://journals.plos.org/plosmedicine/article?id=10.1371/journal.pmed.1000316.

13. John T. Cacioppo and William Patrick, *Loneliness, Human Nature and the Need for Social Connection* (New York: W. W. Norton, 2009).

14. Emily Gurnon, "What Loneliness Is Doing to Your Heart," Next Avenue, July 8, 2016, http://www.nextavenue.org/loneliness-linked-greater-risk-heart-attack-stroke.

15. "Aging Baby Boomers, Childless and Unmarried, at Risk of Becoming Elder Orphans," Northwell Health Newsroom, Northwell Health, May 15 2015, https://www.northwell.edu/about/news/aging-baby-boomers-childless-and-unmarried-risk-becoming-elder-orphans.

16. "Women and Caregivers: Facts and Figures," Family Caregiver Alliance, National Center of Caregiving, https://www.caregiver.org/women-and-caregiving-facts-and-figures.

17. Demand Institute, *Baby Boomers & Their Homes on Their Own Terms* (2013), http://demandinstitute.org/demandwp/wp-content/uploads/2014/12/baby-boomers-and-their-homes.pdf.

18. "Livable Communities Baby Boomer Facts and Figures," Livable Communities, Great Places for All Ages, AARP, April 2014, http://www.aarp.org/livable-communities/info-2014/livable-communities-facts-and-figures.html.

19. Neil Howe, "The Graying of Wealth," *Forbes*, March 16, 2018, https://www.forbes.com/sites/neilhowe/2018/03/16/the-graying-of-wealth/.

20. Tim Mulaney, "Innovater, Bill Thomas Introduces MAGIC Housing Model," Senior Housing News, November 27, 2017, https://seniorhousingnews.com/2017/11/27/senior-living-innovator-bill-thomas-introduces-magic-housing-model/.

21. "Convents Around the Area, Country Close as Nuns Age, Numbers Dwindle." CBS New York, May 16, 2017, http://newyork.cbslocal.com/2017/05/17/nuns-convents-closing/.

22. Aldersgate residents participate as voting members on the board and all board committees including the strategic planning and master site planning committees to assure their voices and active participation in decision-making.

23. D'Vera Cohn, "A record 64 million Americans live in multigenerational households," Pew Research Center, April 2018, http://www.pewresearch .org/fact-tank/2018/04/05/a-record-64-million-americans-live-in-multi generational-households/?amp=1.
24. Marcie Geffner, "Buying a Home with Family: How to Start," Bankrate, http://www.bankrate.com/finance/real-estate/buying-a-home-with-family .aspx.
25. Chris Kirkham, "Hurdles to Multigenerational Living: Kitchens and Visible Second Entrances," *Wall Street Journal*, March 14, 2016, https://accessory dwellings.org/adu-regulations-by-city/.
26. Michael Lerner, "Demand Rise for Properties That Can House More Than One Generation," *Washington Post*, September 30, 2015, https://www .washingtonpost.com/realestate/demand-rising-for-properties-that-can -house-more-than-one-generation/2015/09/29/9d6f7042-50b d-11e5-8c19 -0b6825aa4a3a_story.html.
27. US Census Bureau, *Median and Average Sale Price of New Homes Sold in the U.S.* (2016), https://www.census.gov/construction/nrs/pdf/usprice mon.pdf.
28. Benjy Hansen-Bundy, "A Week Inside WeLive, the Utopian Apartment Complex That Wants to Disrupt City Living," *GQ*, February 27, 2018, https://www.gq.com/story/inside-welive/amp.

Chapter 12: Strategic Responses to Housing

1. "Less Is More: The Tiny House Movement Infographic," Custom Made, August 8, 2014, https://www.custommade.com/blog/tiny-house-movement/.
2. Adele Peters, "This Village of Tiny Houses Is Giving Seattle's Homeless a Place to Live," *Fast Company*, January 26, 2016, https://www.fastcoexist .com/3055771/change-generation/this-village-of-tiny-houses-is-giving -seattles-homeless-a-place-to-live.
3. Erin Carlyle, "Ultra-Posh Tiny Homes: The Small House Movement Goes Lux," *Forbes*, February 17, 2015, http://www.forbes.com/sites/erincarlyle /2015/02/17/ultra-posh-tiny-homes-the-small-house-movement-goes-luxe /2/#50d065db71c6.
4. Emily Badger, "The Next Big Fight over Housing Could Happen Literally in Your Backyard," *Washington Post*, August 7, 2016, https://www.washing tonpost.com/news/wonk/wp/2016/08/07/why-building-a-home-on-your -own-land-has-become-so-controversial/.

5. *Cohousing in the United States: An Innovative Model of Sustainable Neigh-borhoods*, Cohousing Association of the United States, April 2016, https://www.amazon.com/Cohousing-Contemporary-Approach-Housing-Our selves/dp/0898155398.

6. *12 Characteristics of Cohousing Communities*, MidAtlanticCohousing.org, 2015, http://www.midatlanticcohousing.org/uploads/5/7/9/8/57982291/top_12_characteristics_of_cohousing.pdf.

7. The Cohousing Association of the United States, www.cohousing.org/directory.

8. Genevieve Rajewski, "Developer Takes Novel Approach to Senior Housing," Affordable Housing Finance, August 1, 2007, http://www.housingfinance.com/news/developer-takes-novel-approach-to-seniors-housing_o.

9. Alice Green, "Update on My Progress on New Paths," Aging in Community, August 13, 2016, http://www.agingincommunity.com/help-alice_the_original_petition.

10. Ann Zabaldo, "Cohousing & HUD: A Love Story," Cohousing Association of the United States, June 12, 2014, http://www.cohousing.org/node/2290.

Index